NAUGHTY
CATTITUDE COLORING BOOK
HIKARU KOTZ

HIKARU KOTZ

THANK YOU FOR YOUR SUPPORT!

Dear Colorist,

Thank you for choosing my coloring book! I'm delighted to share these pages with you and hope they bring joy and relaxation to your creative journey.

Take your time, let your imagination flow, and most importantly – have fun!

CONNECT WITH ME

I'd love to hear from you! If you have any questions or concerns, please feel free to reach out to me at **hikarukotz@gmail.com**

COPYRIGHT

Copyright © 2025 by Hikaru Kotz. All rights reserved. No part of this publication may be reproduced, distributed, or transmitted in any form or by any means, including photocopying, recording, or other electronic or mechanical methods, without prior written permission from the publisher, except for brief quotations in reviews.

50 FREE COLORING PAGES

As a special thank you for your support, I've prepared something special just for you! Visit our Instagram account to discover over 50 beautiful printable coloring pages waiting for you.

@hikarukotzcoloring

SHARE YOUR BEAUTIFUL ARTWORKS

When you finish coloring, don't hesitate to share your masterpieces on social media and tag **@hikarukotzcoloring**. I'd love to see your creative journey!

BEFORE YOU START...

Amazon's paper is suitable for coloring with colored pencils and alcohol-based markers.

To prevent any potential bleed-through, simply place a sheet of thick paper or card behind the page you are coloring.

A sheet of paper or card

THIS BOOK BELONGS TO

TEST COLOR PAGE

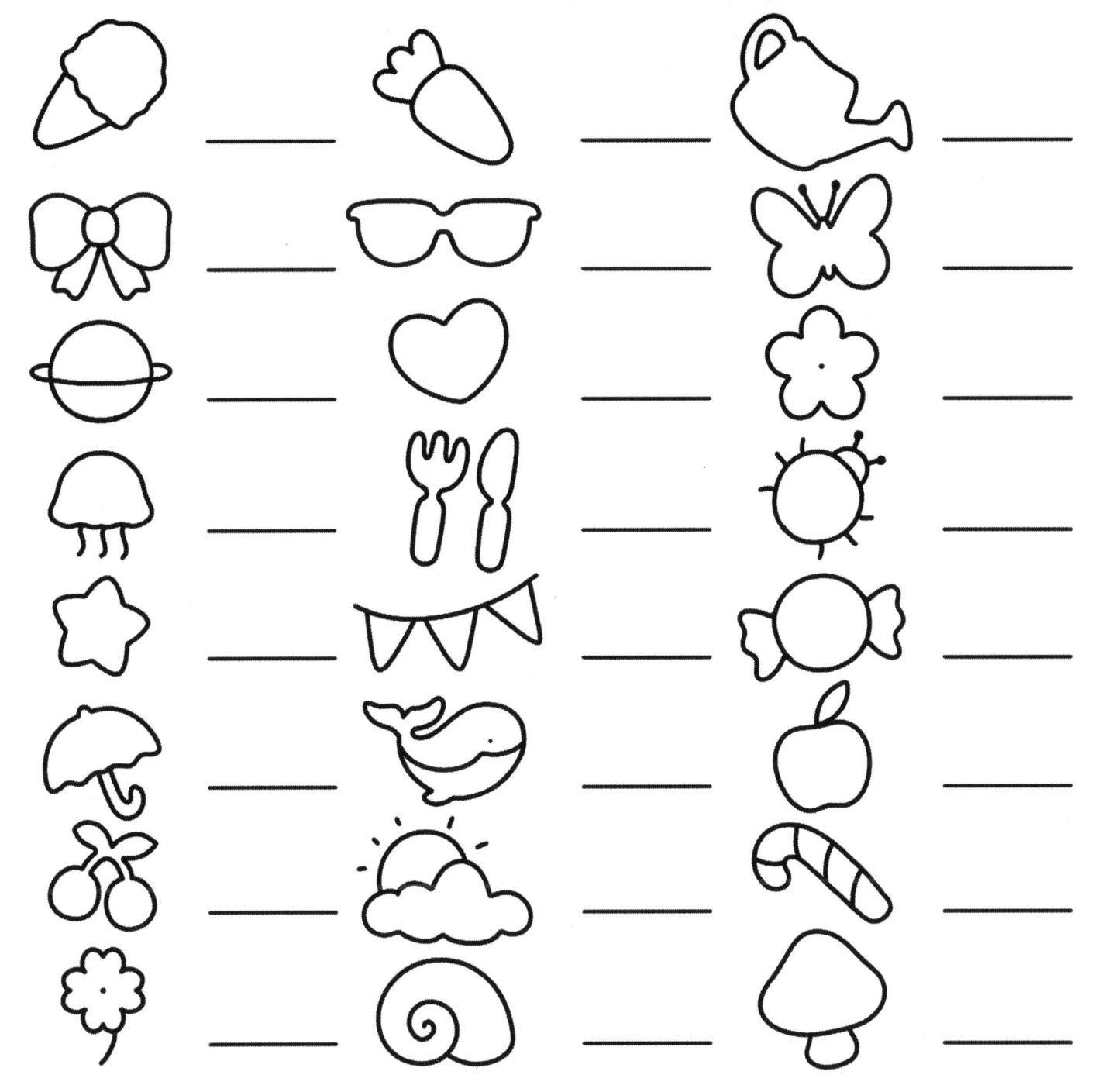

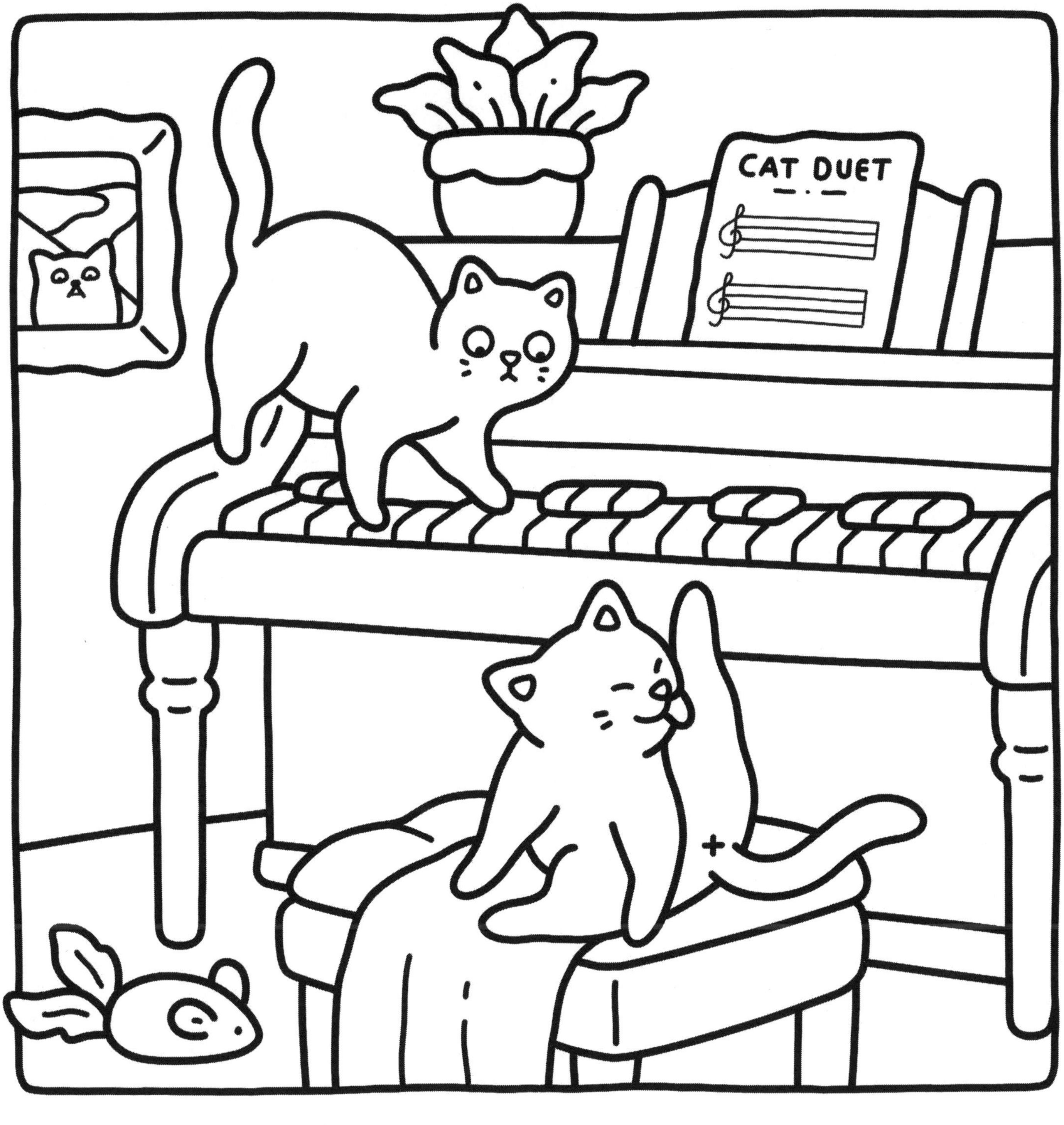
CAT DUET

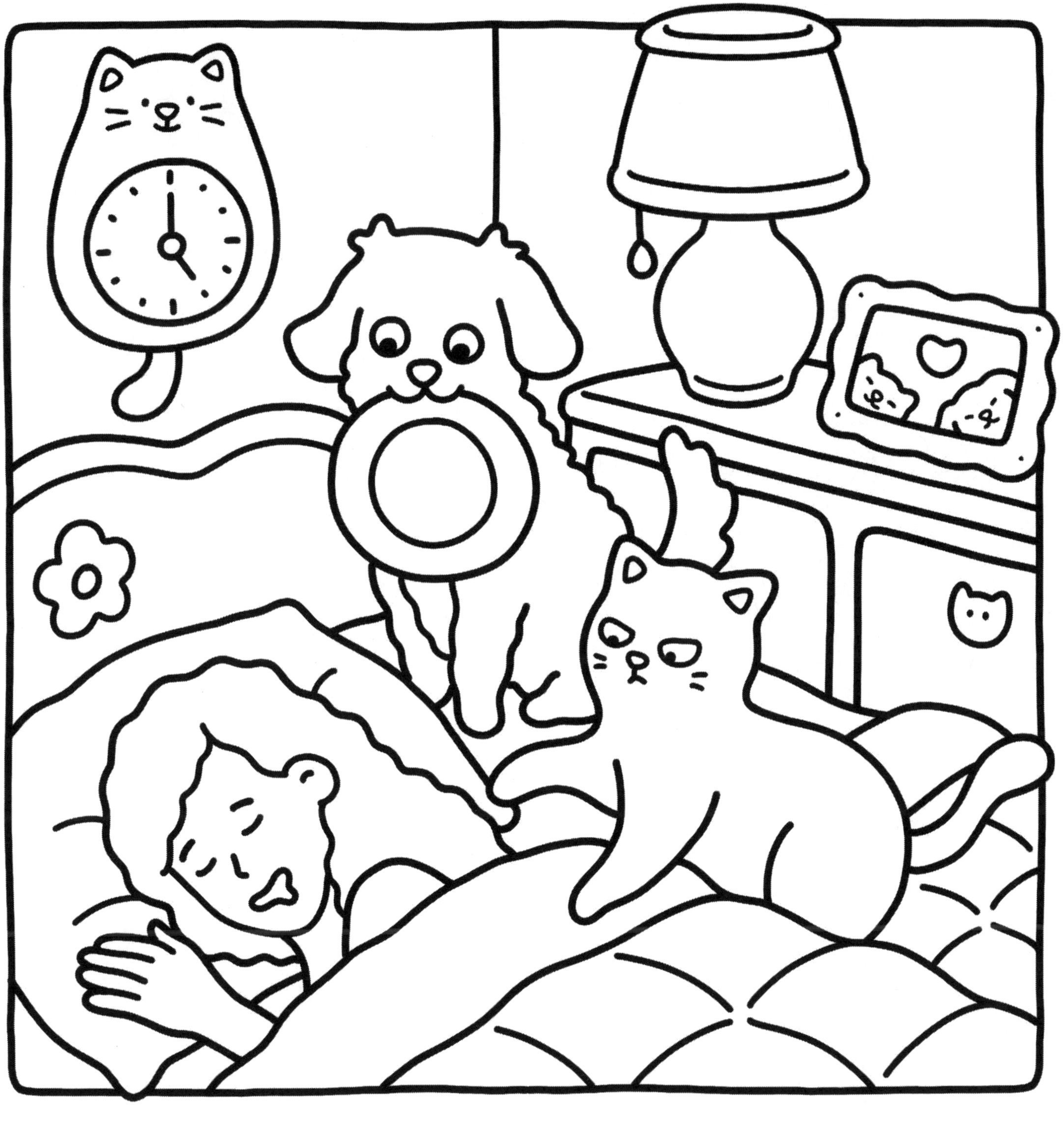

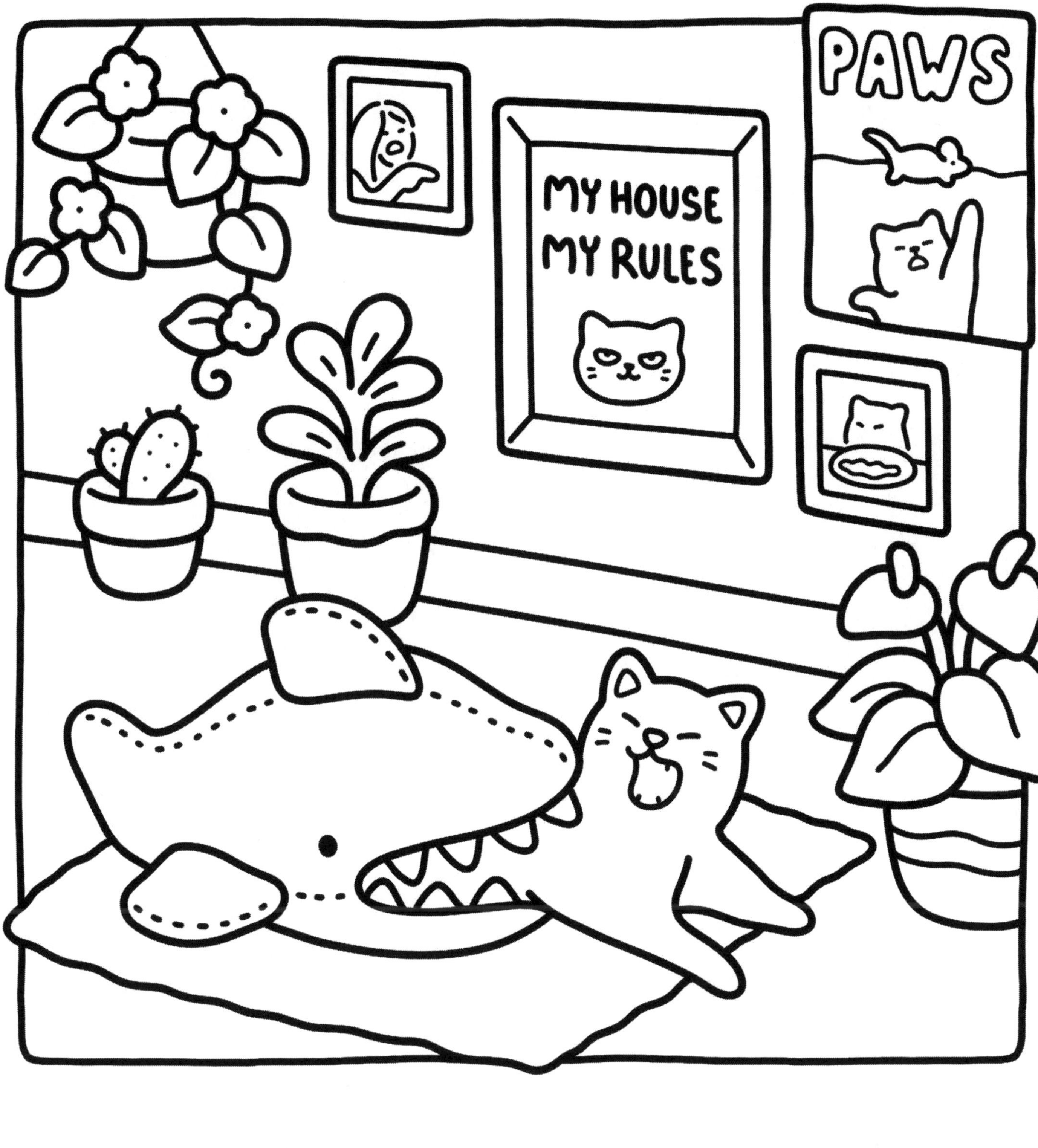
PAWS
MY HOUSE
MY RULES

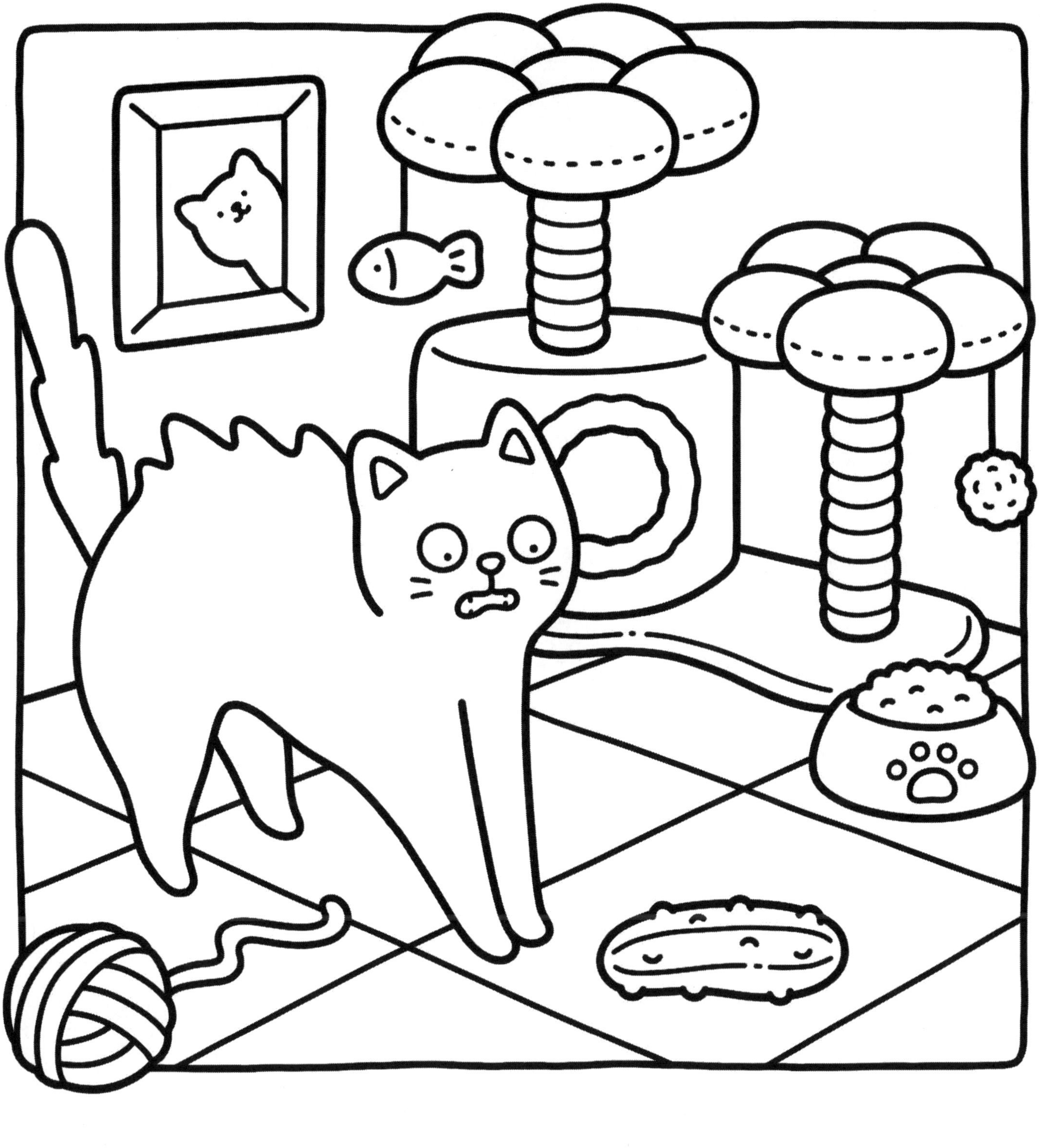

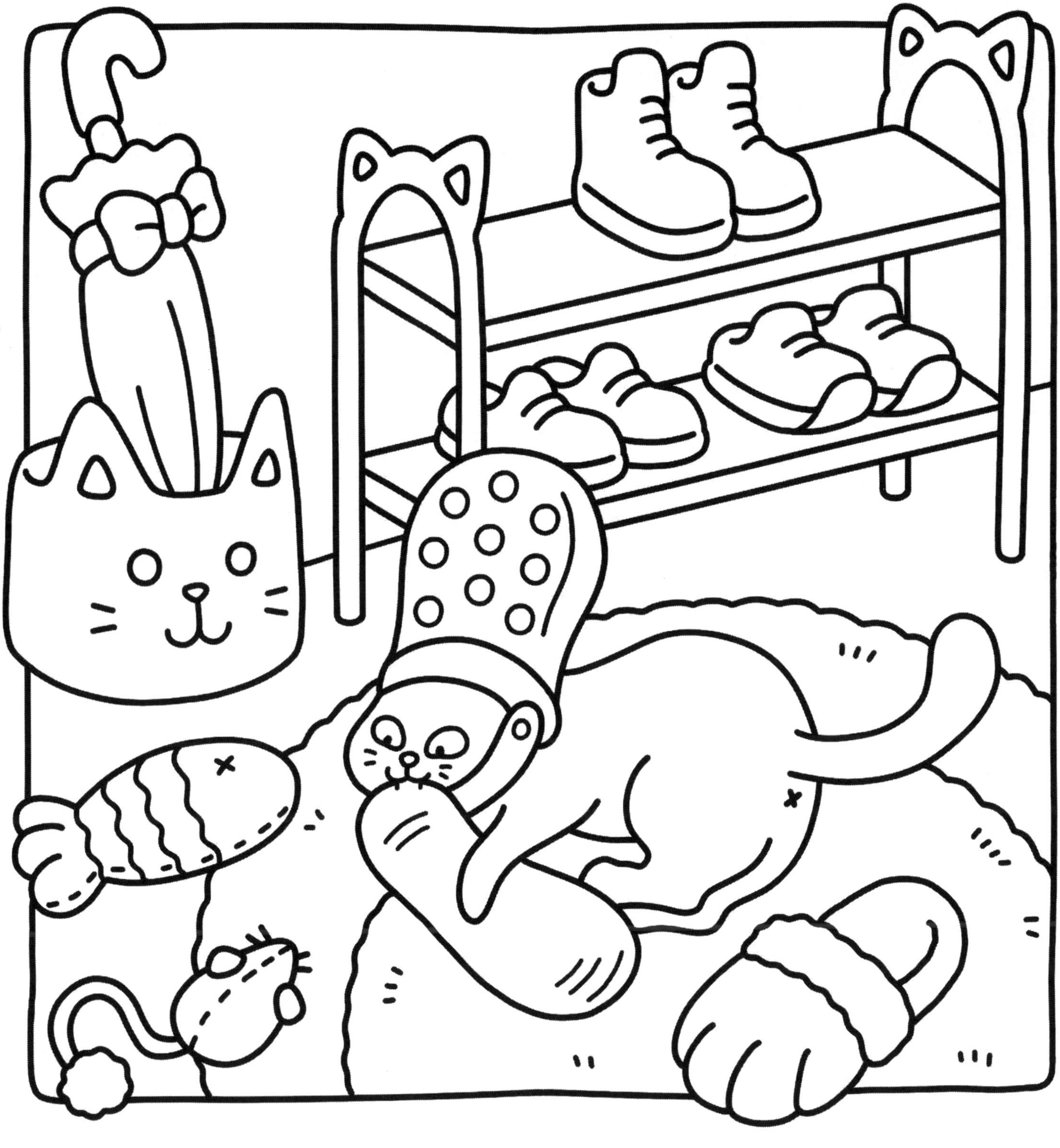

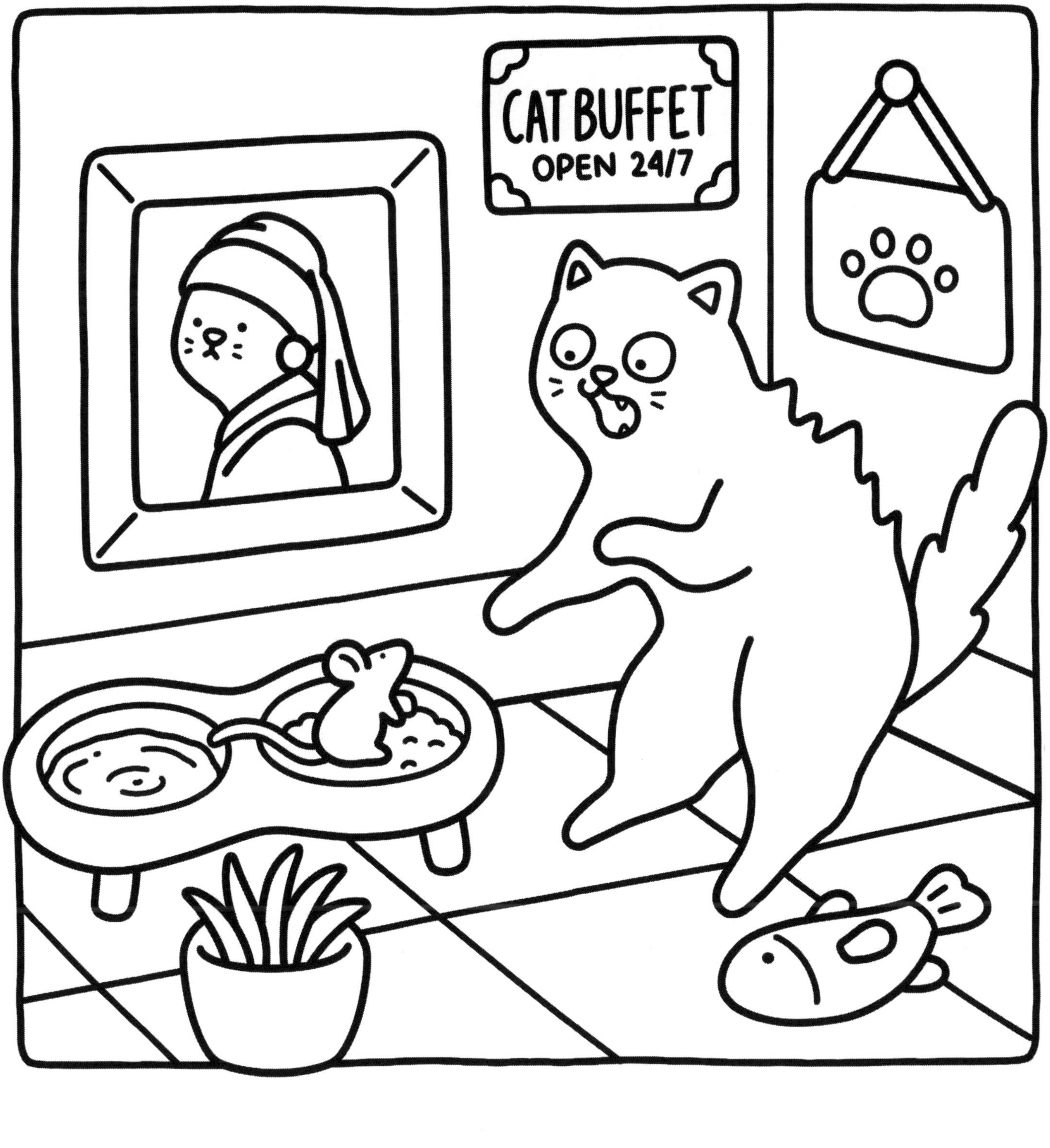
CAT BUFFET
OPEN 24/7

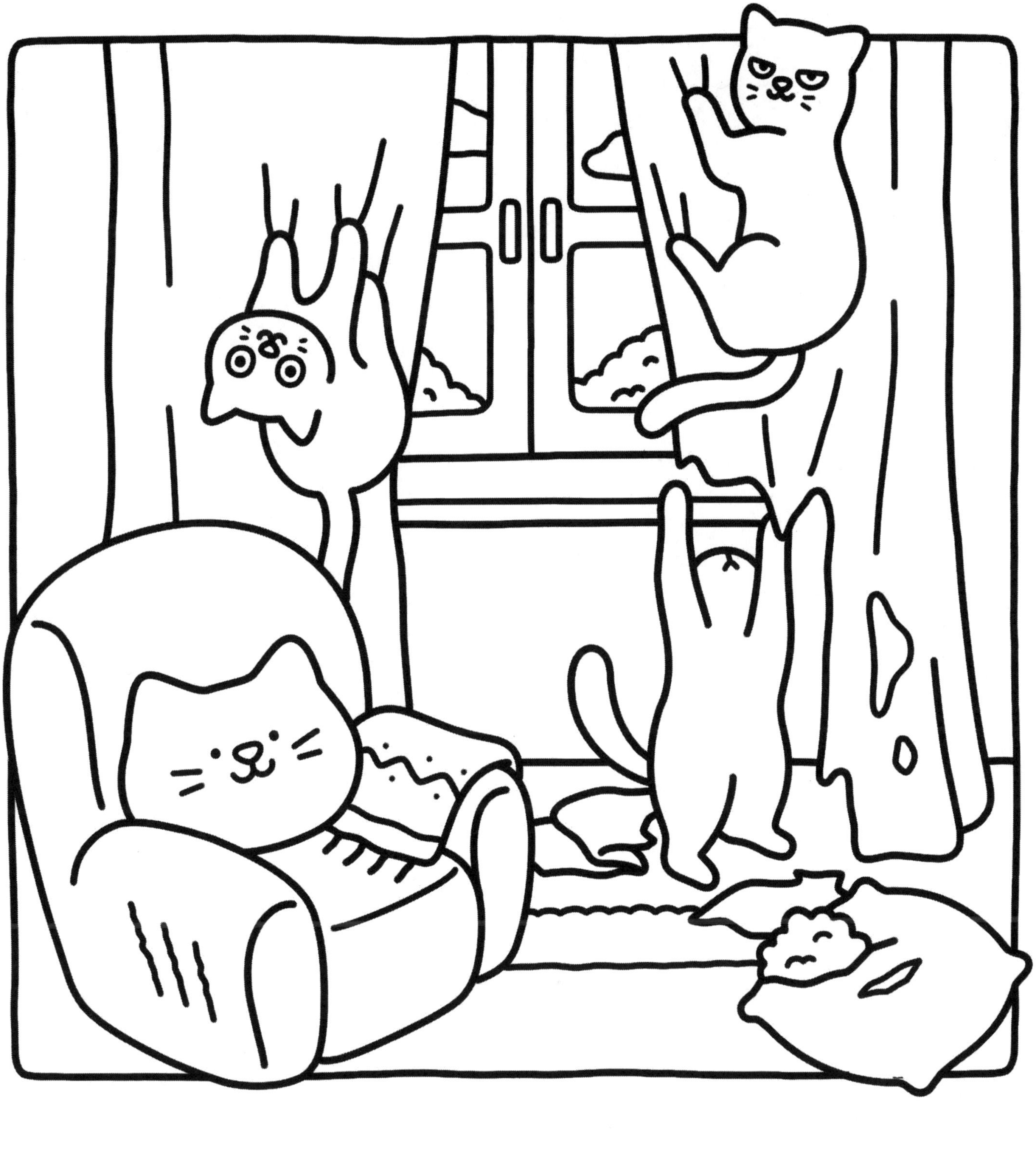

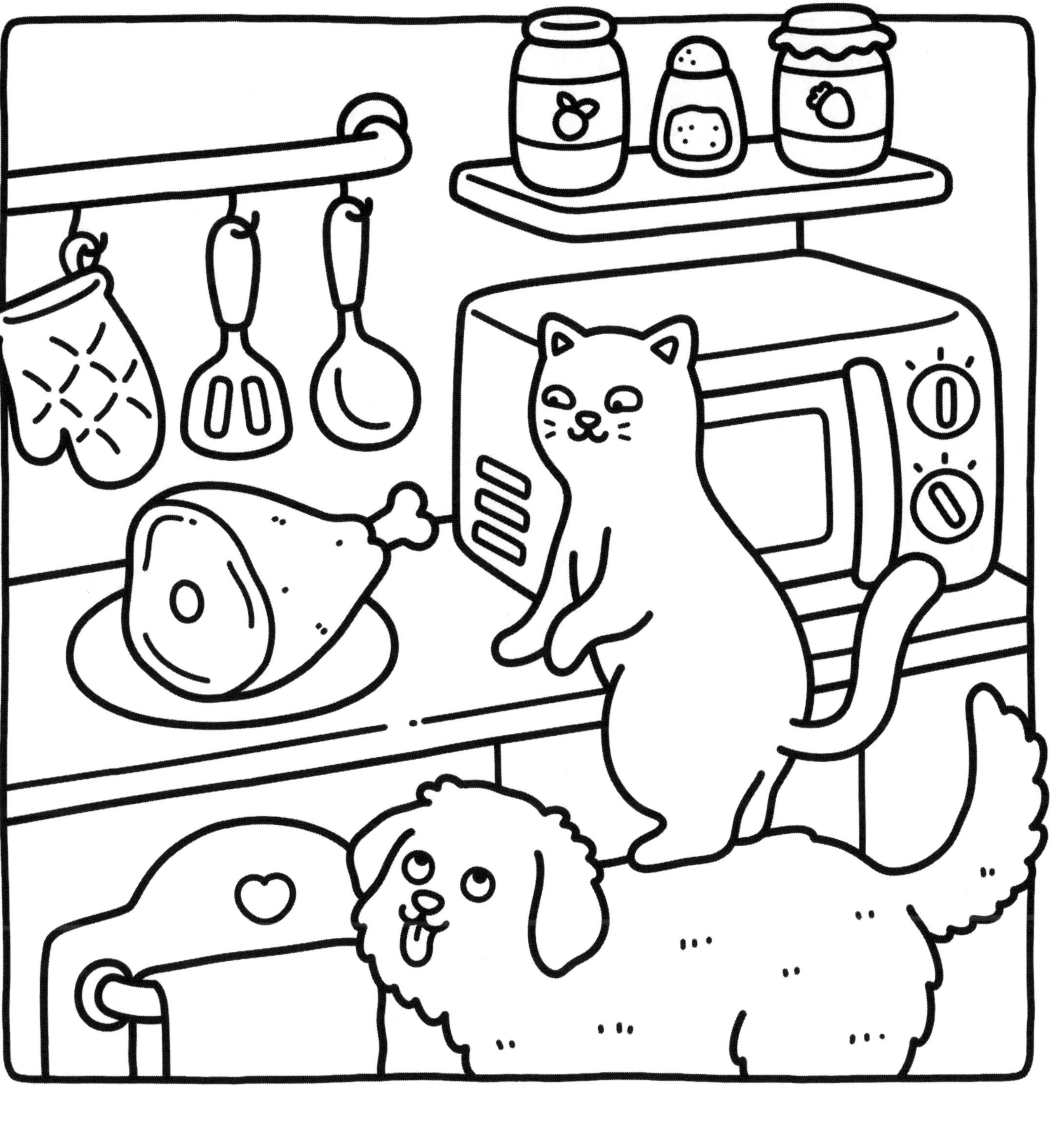

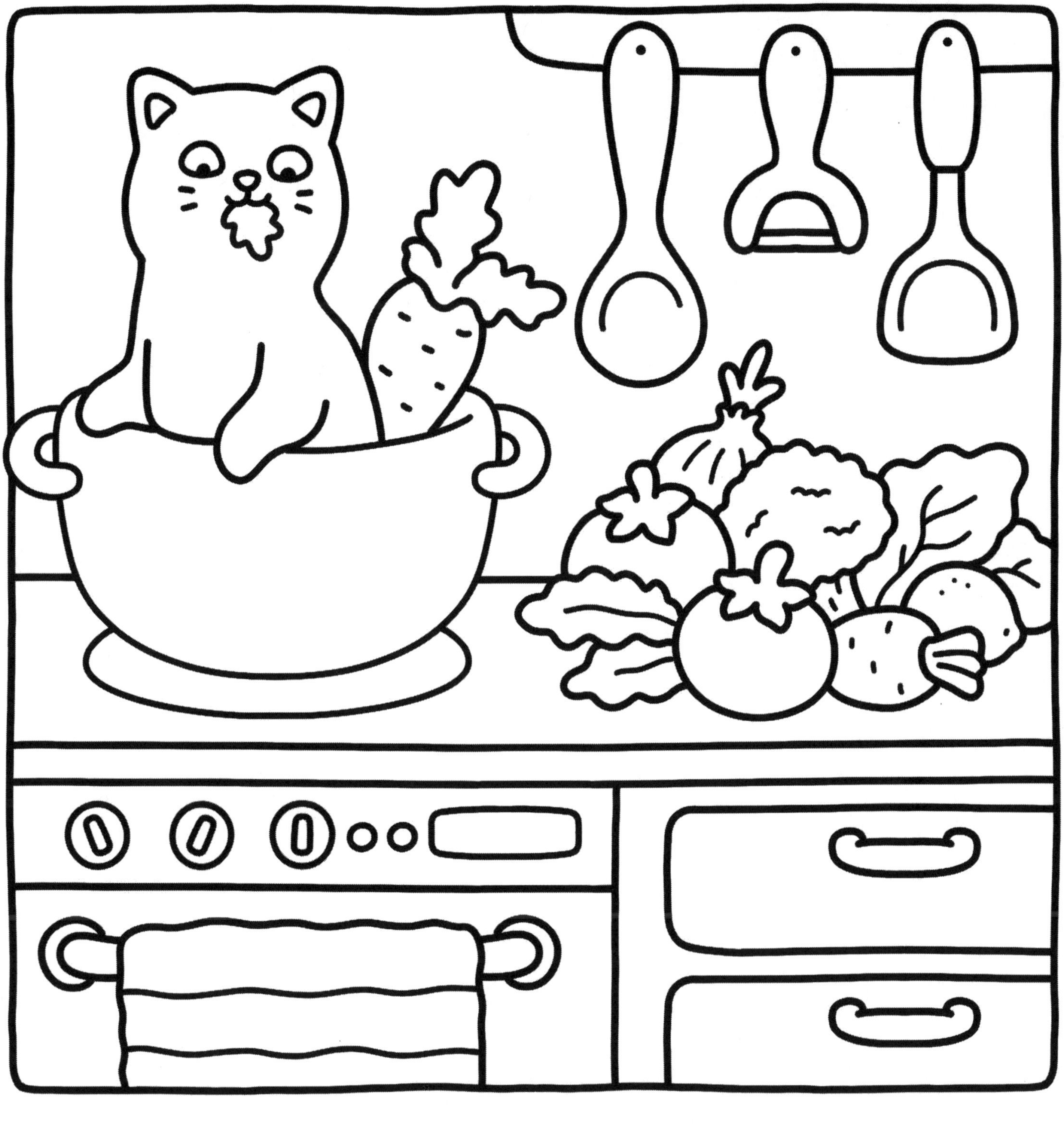

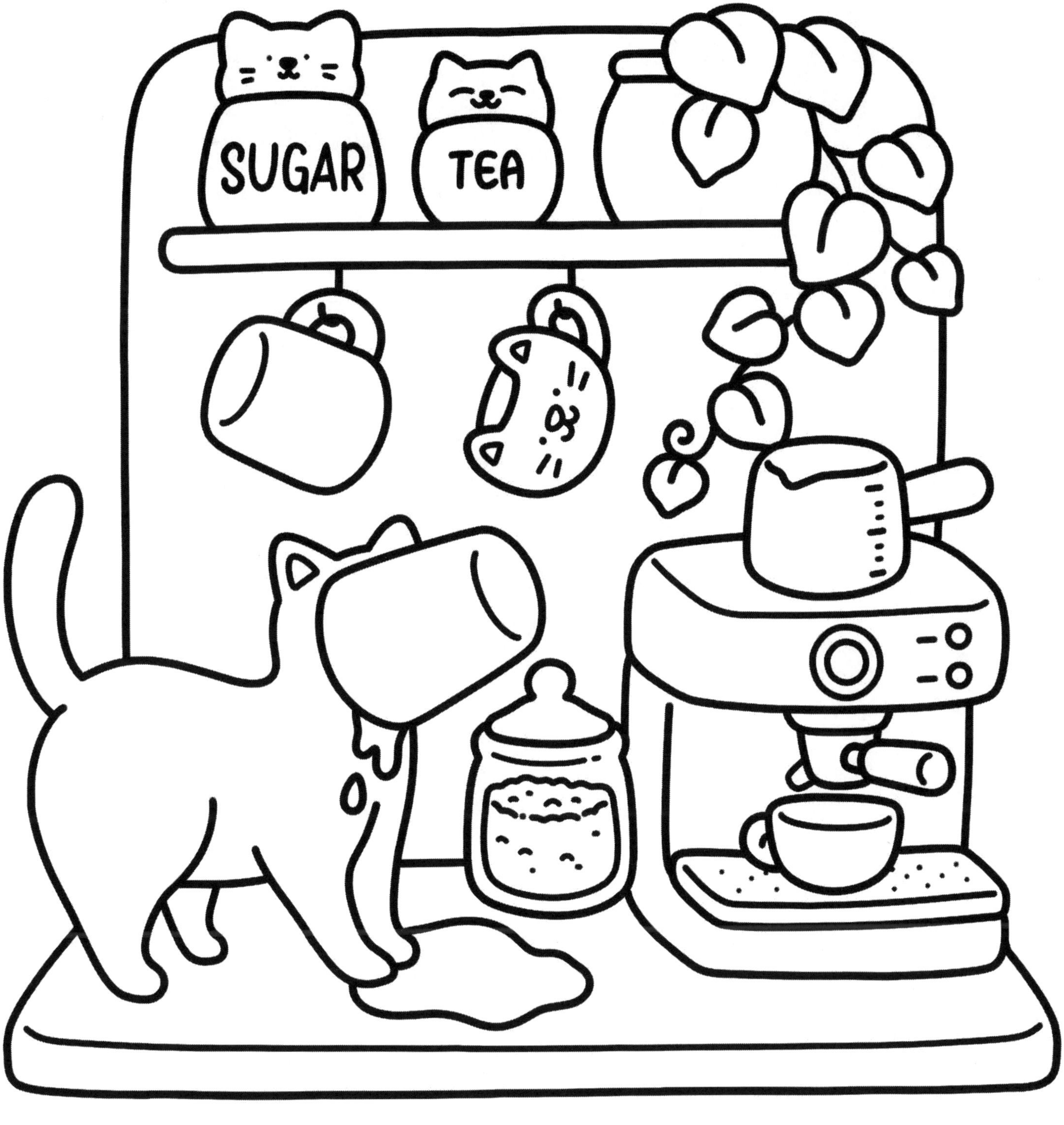
SUGAR
TEA

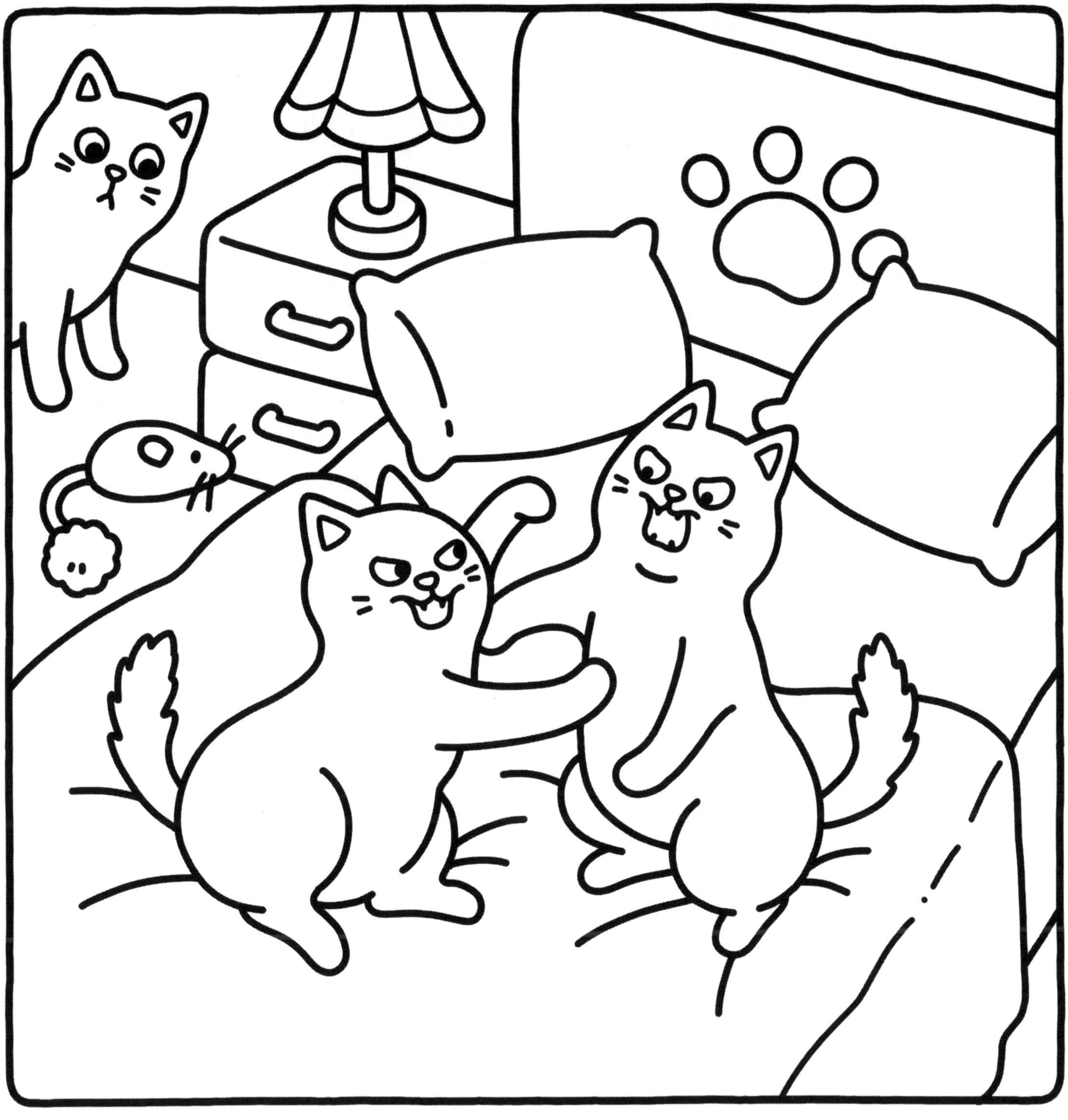

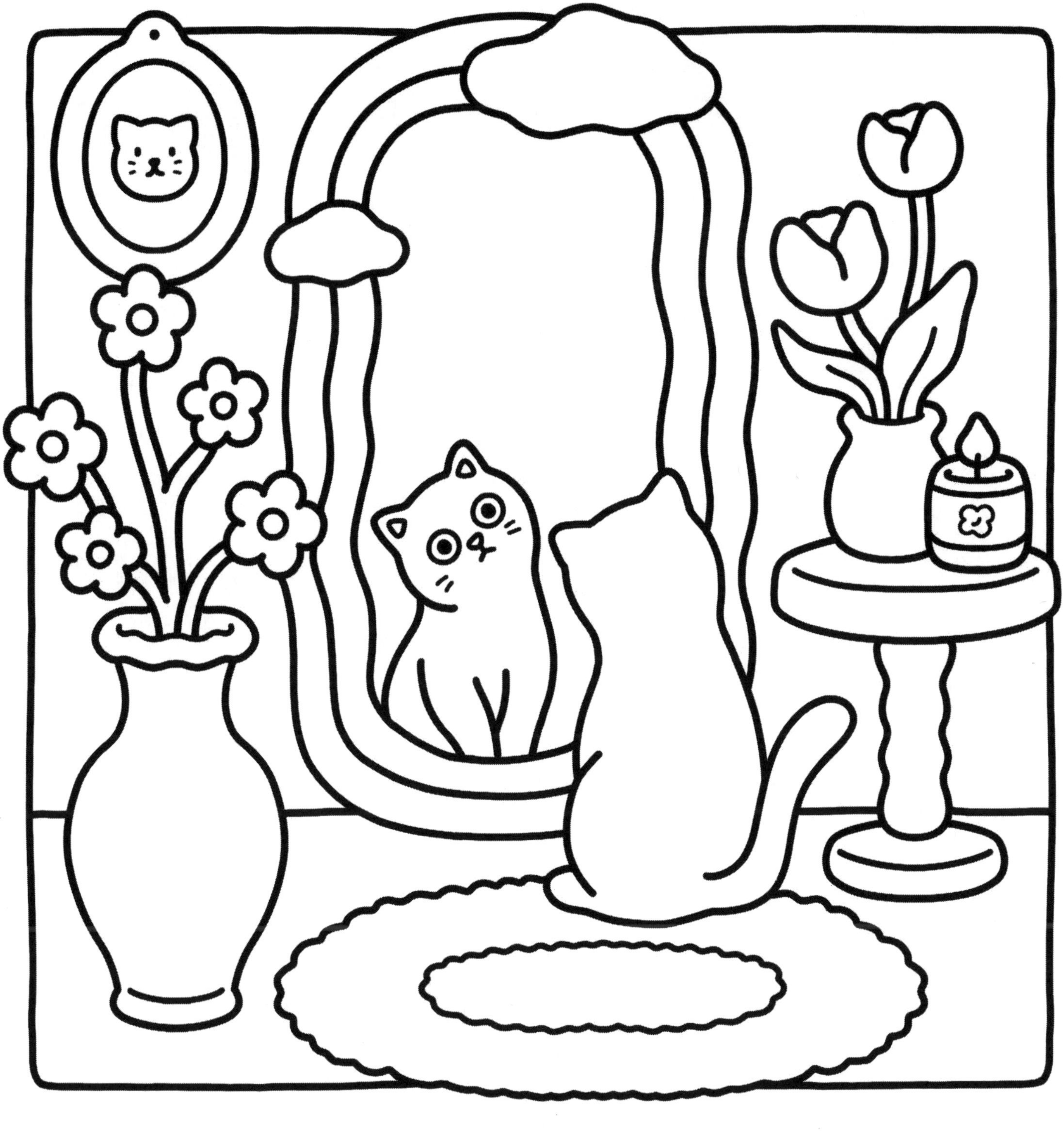

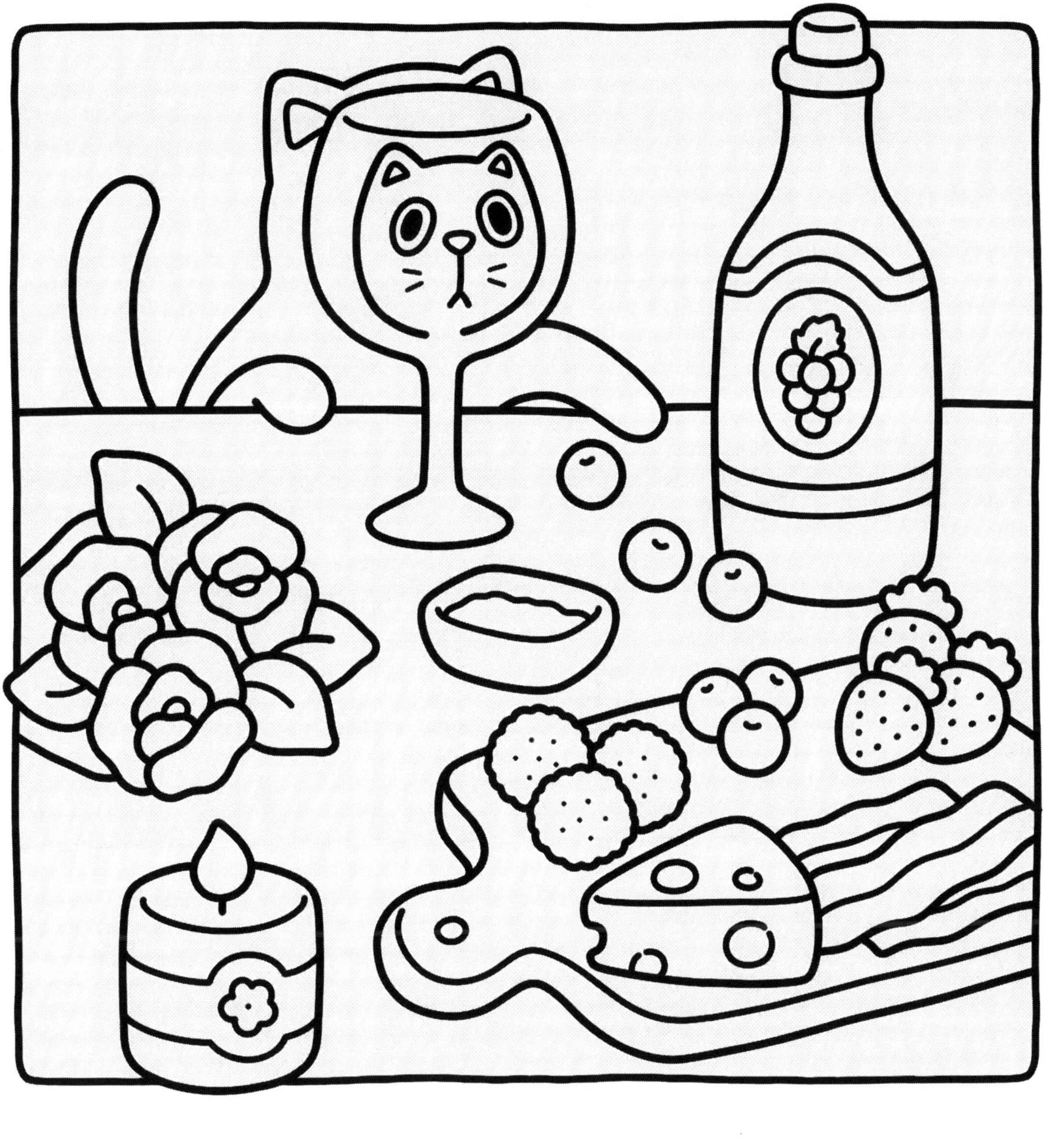

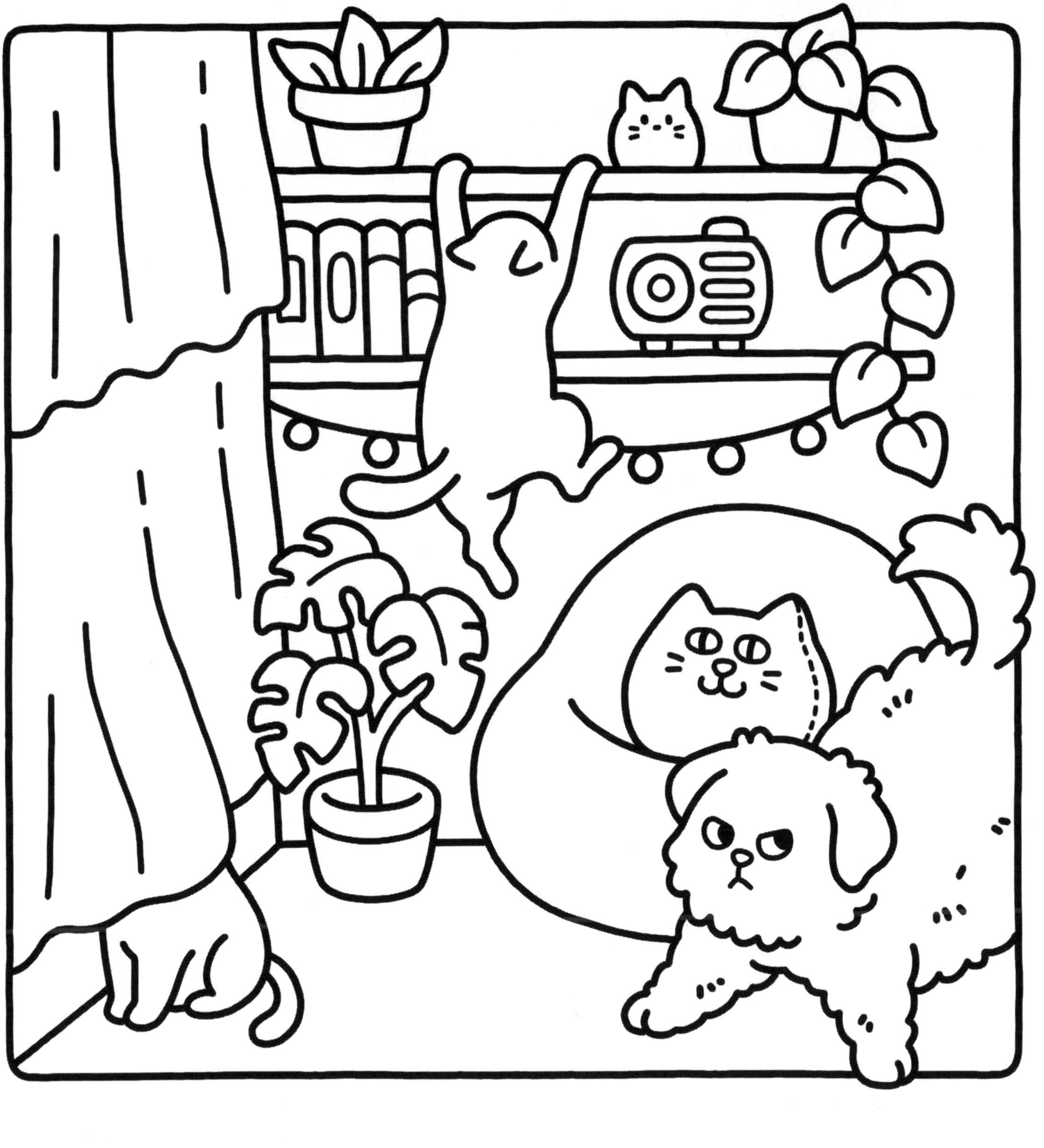

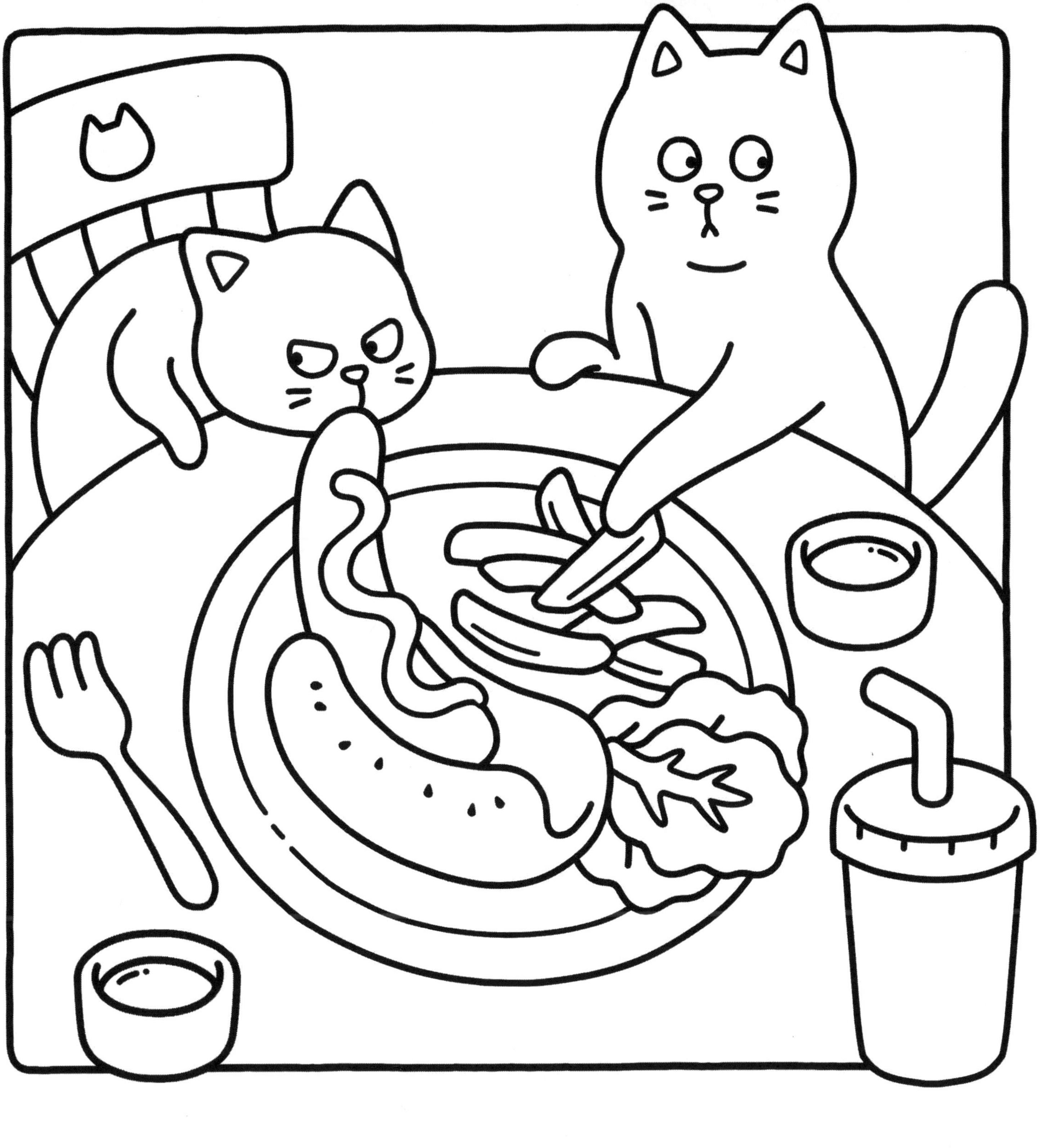

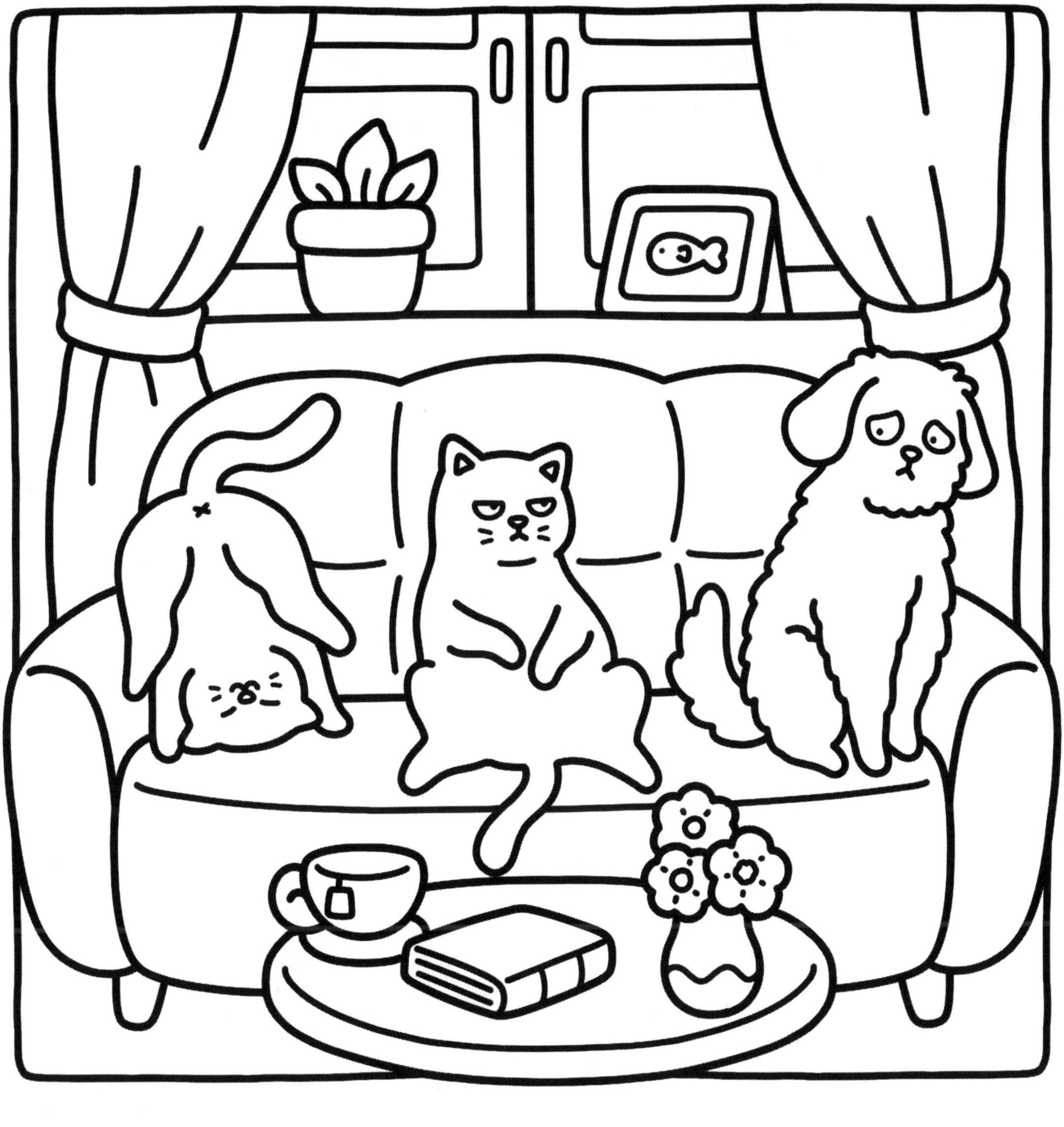

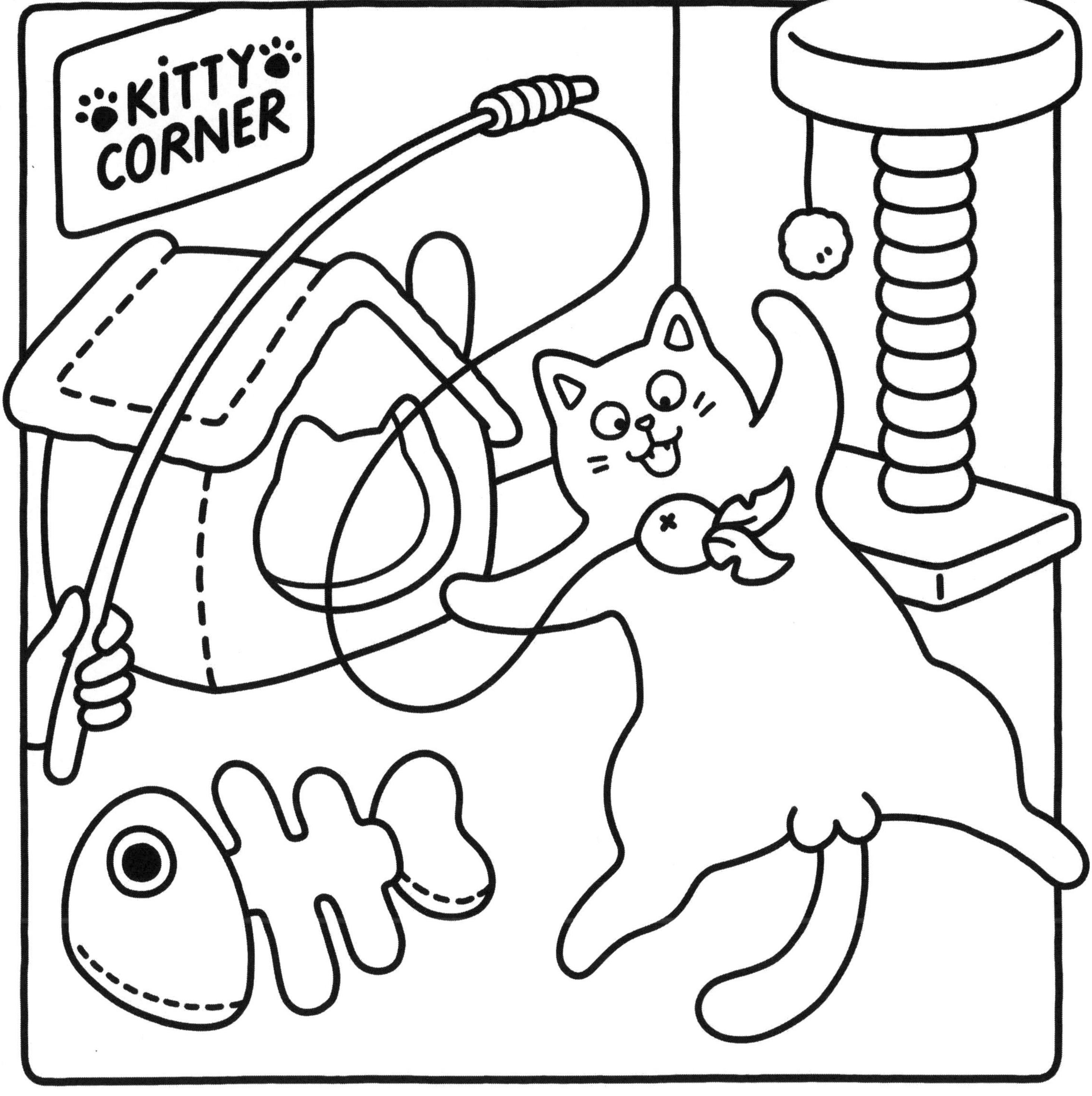
KITTY
CORNER

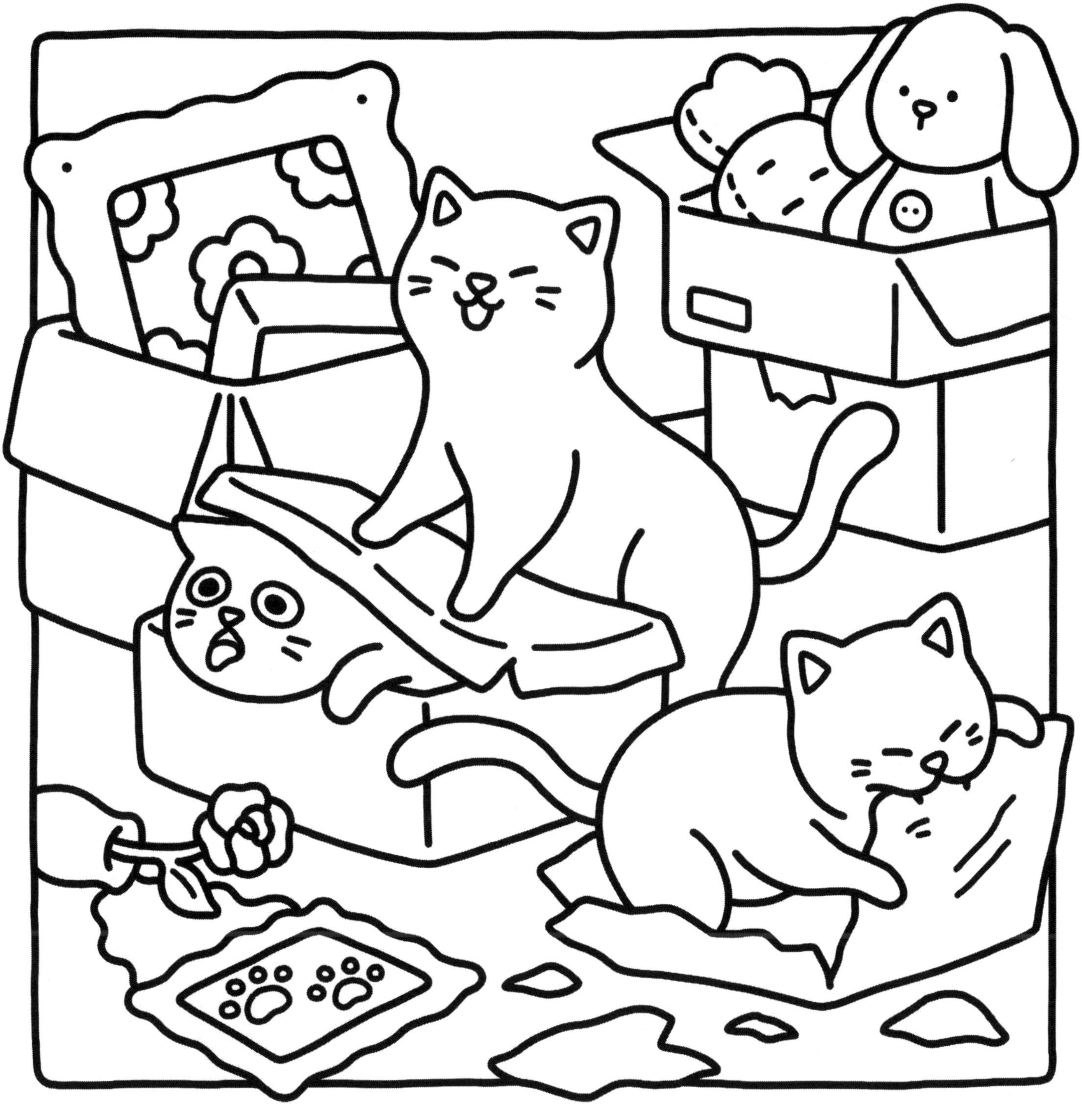

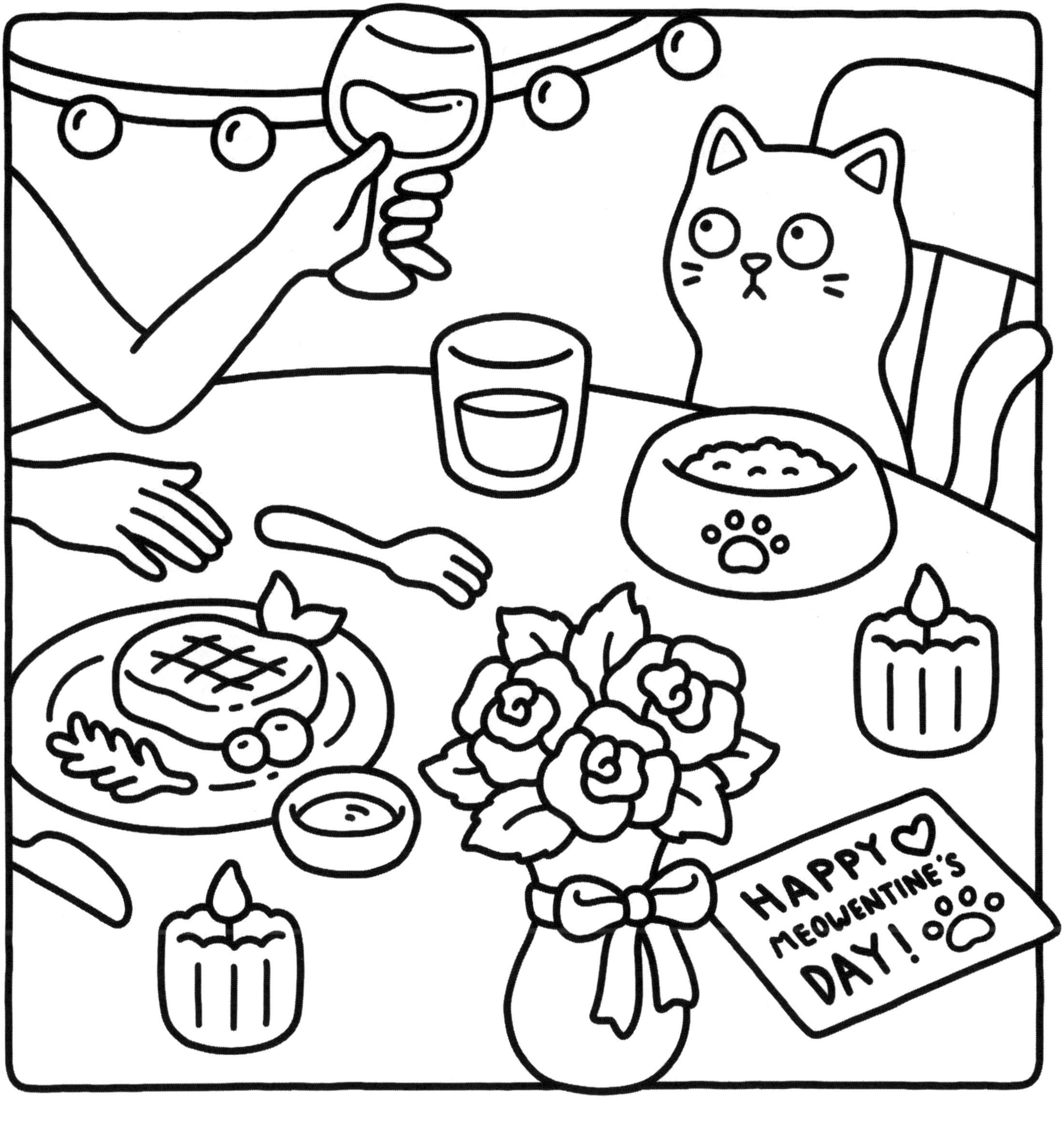
HAPPY
MEOWENTINE'S
DAY!

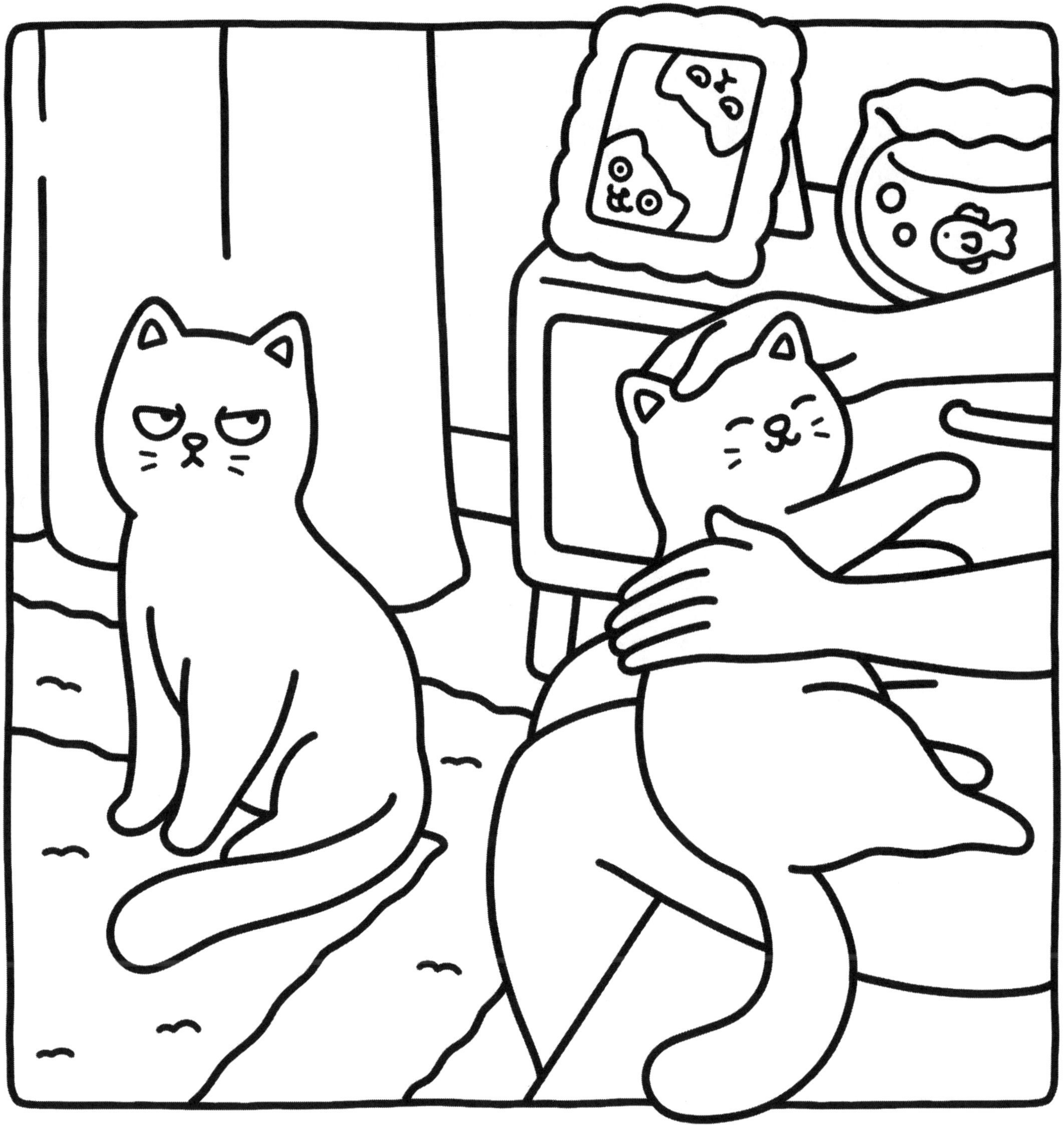

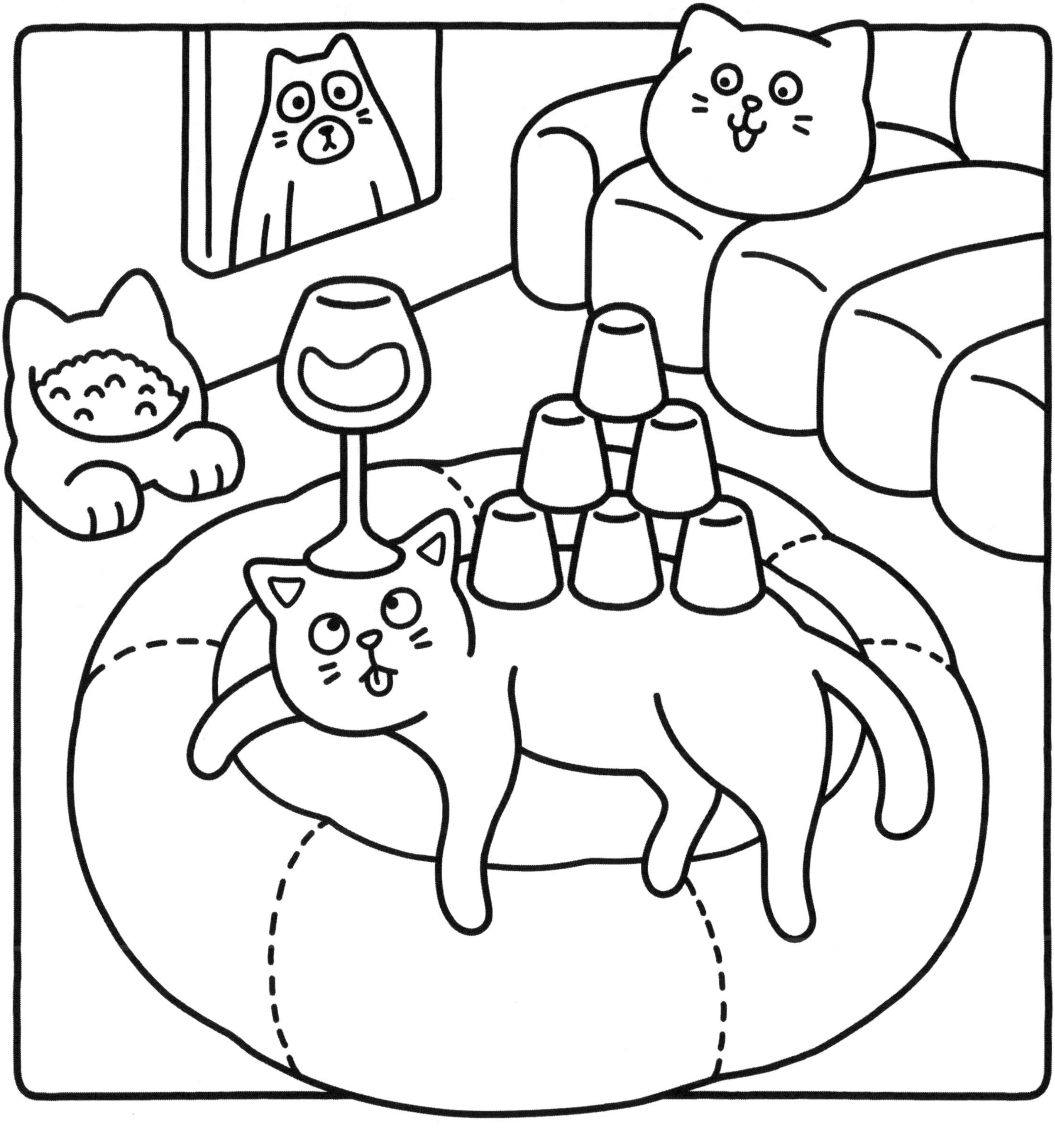

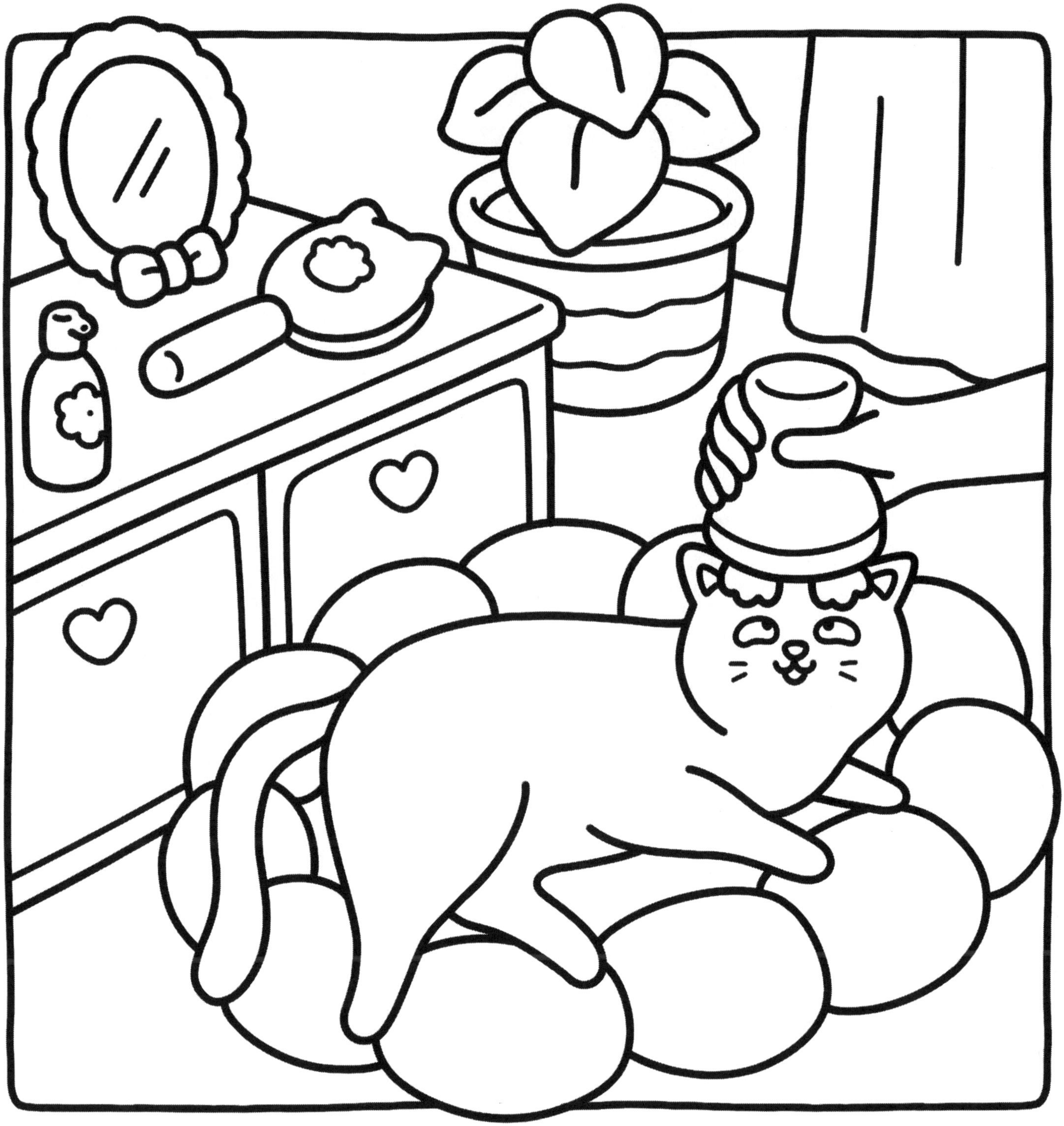

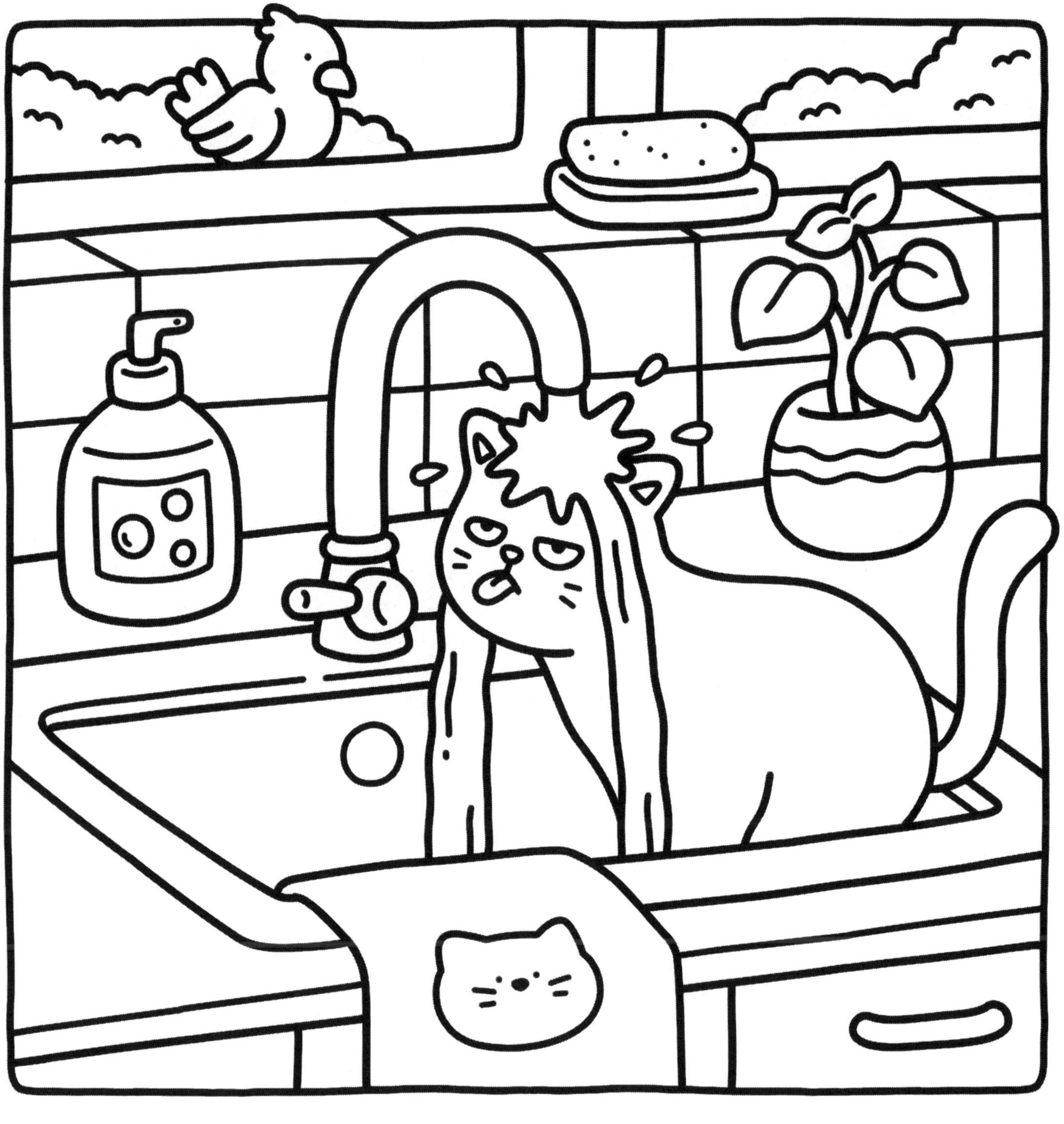

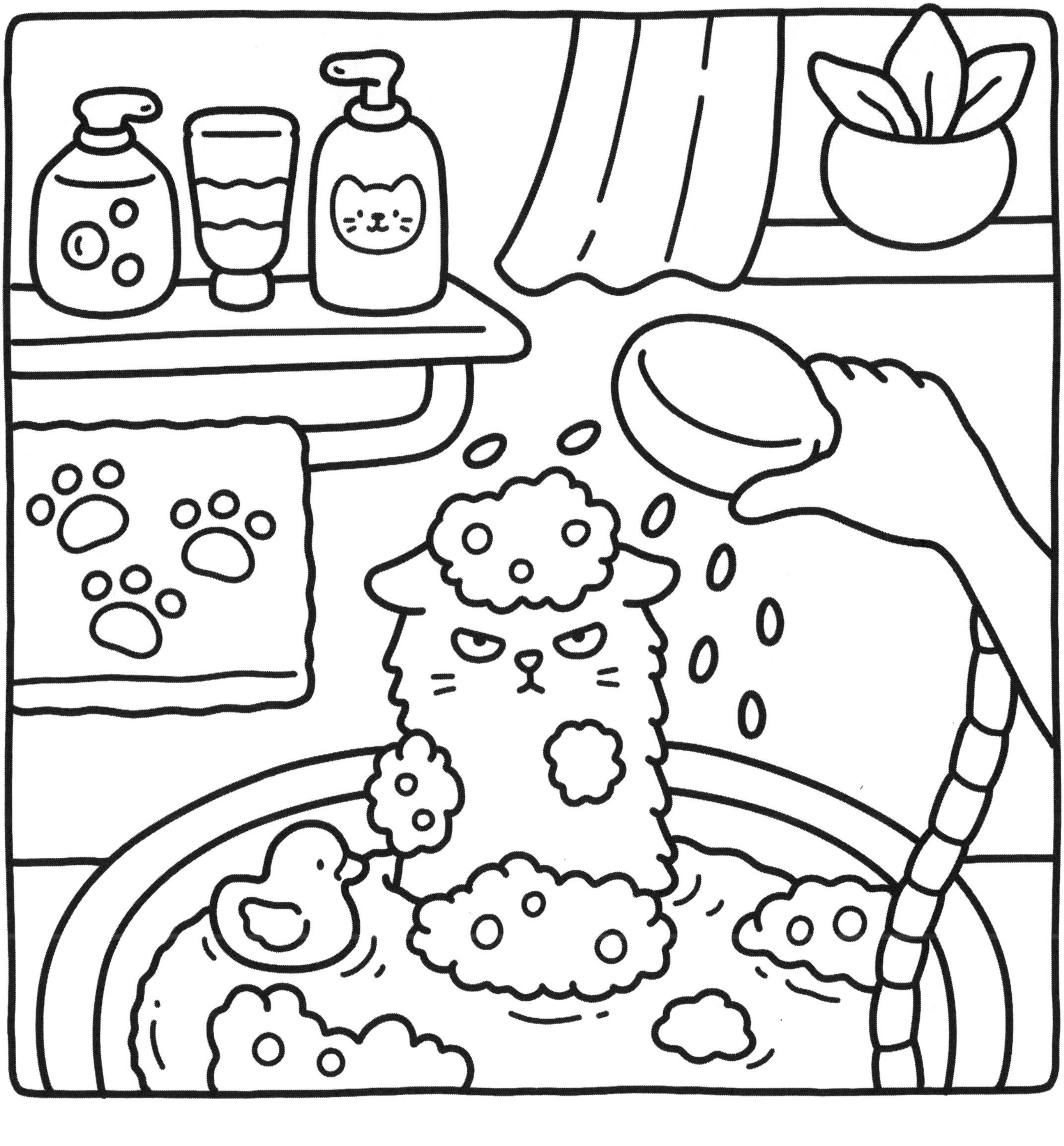

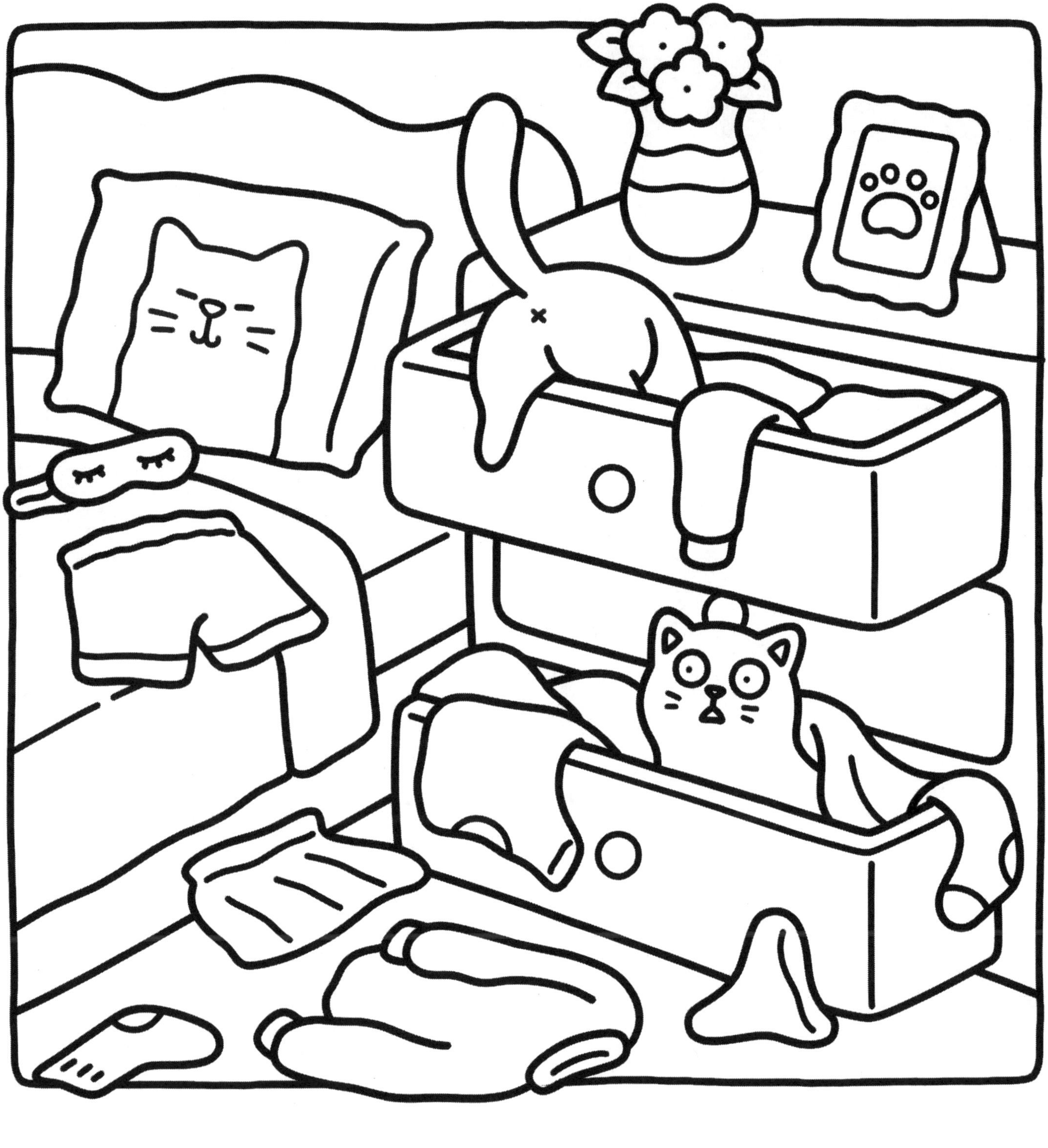

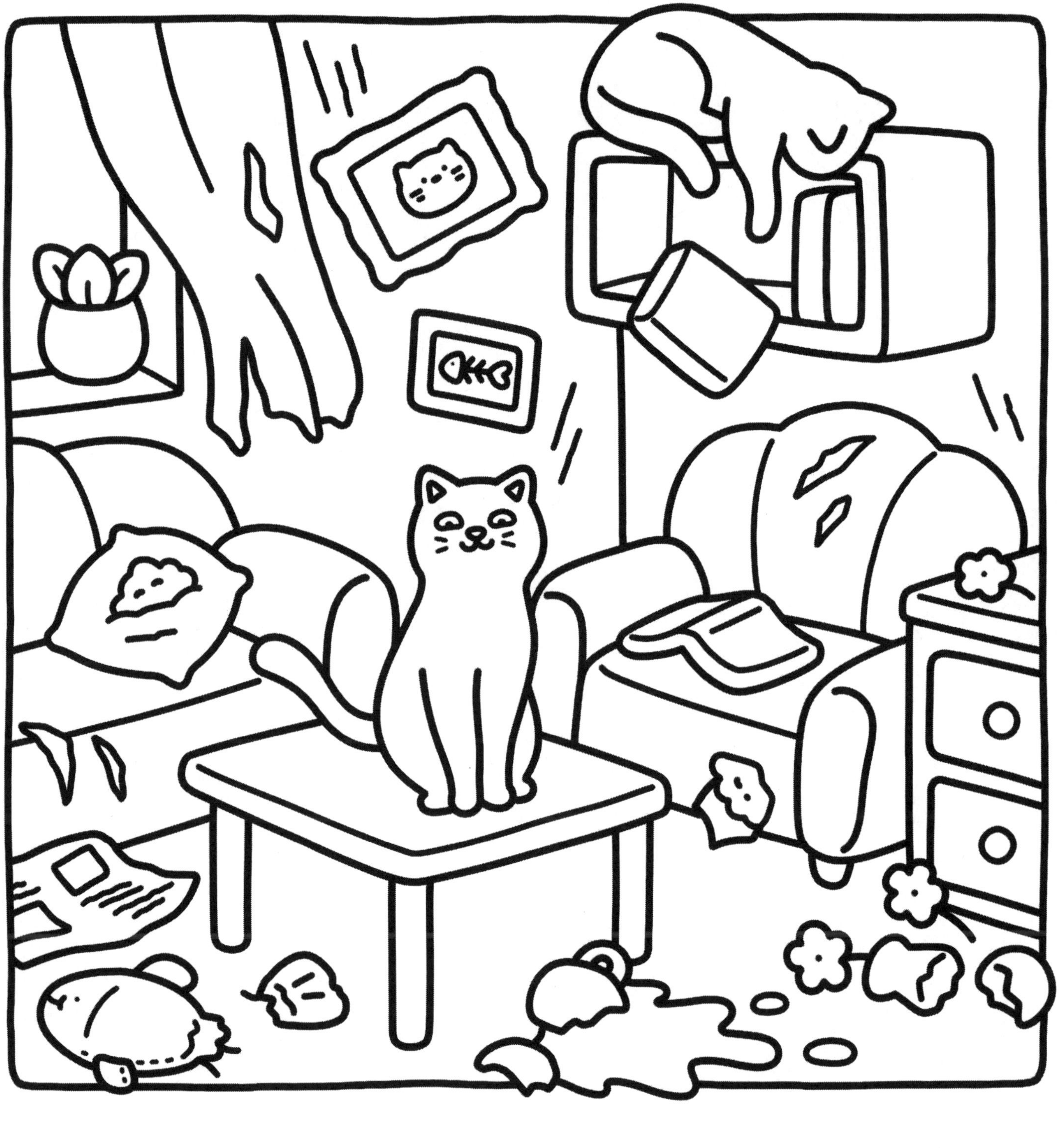

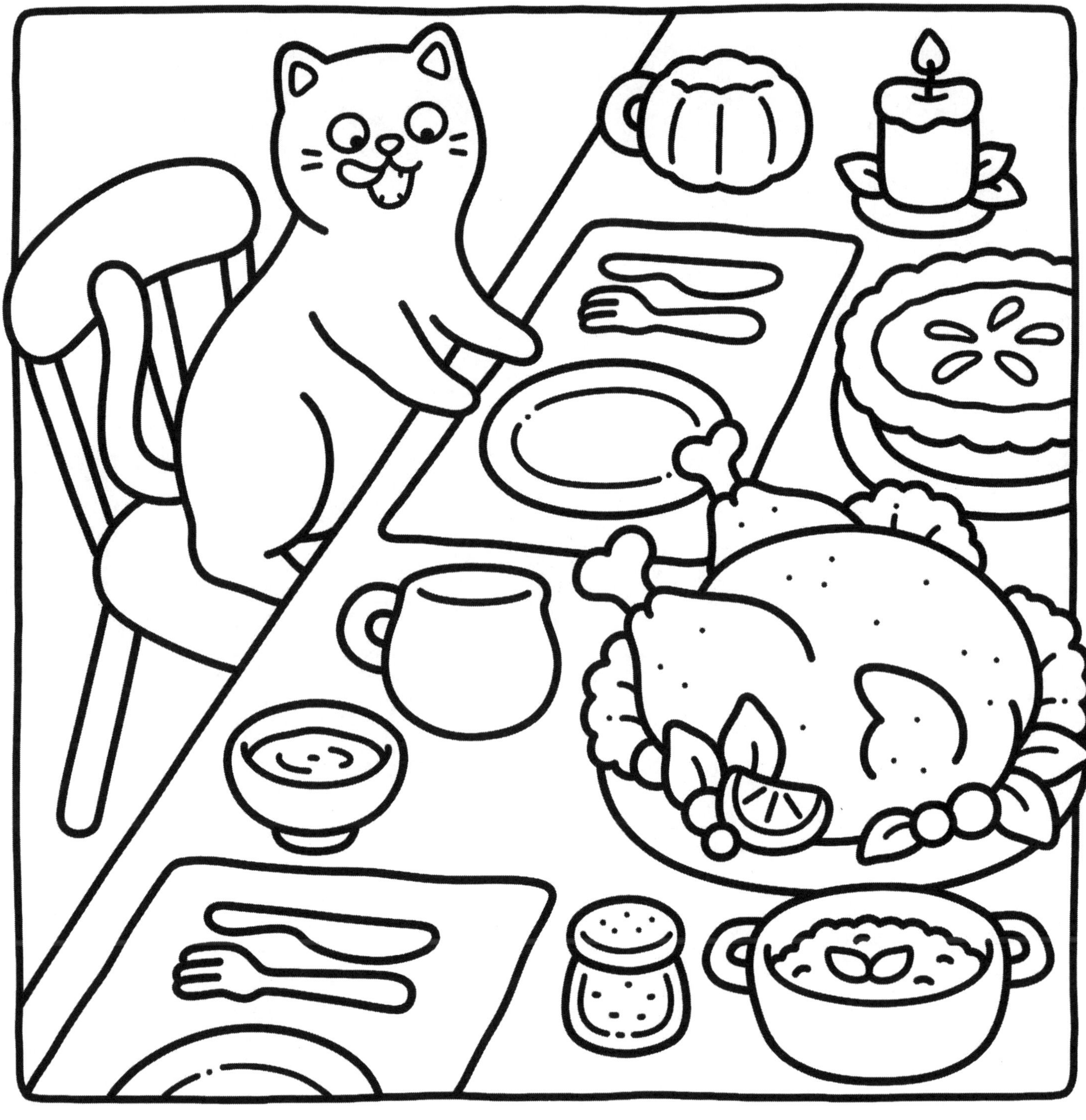

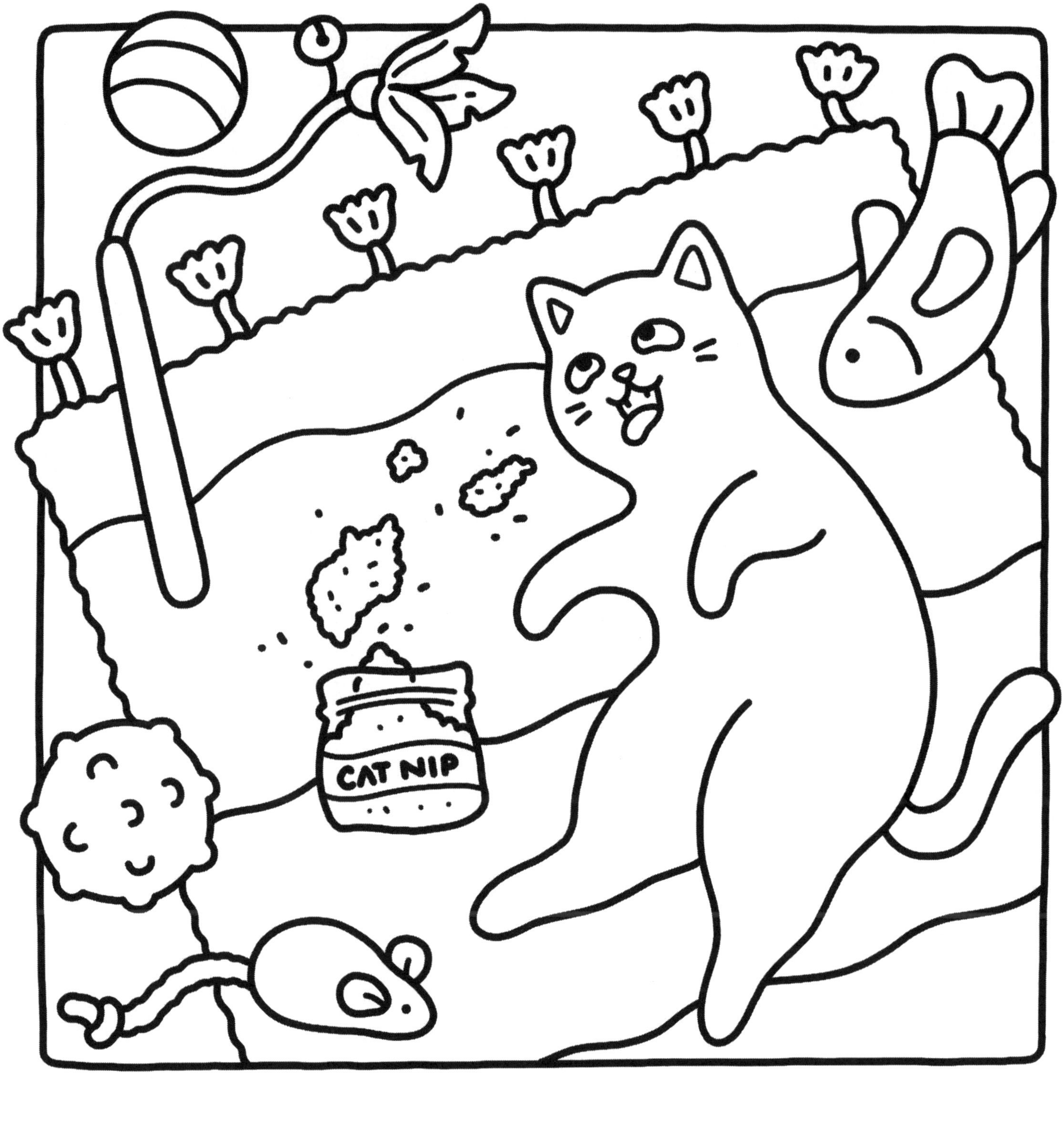
CAT NIP

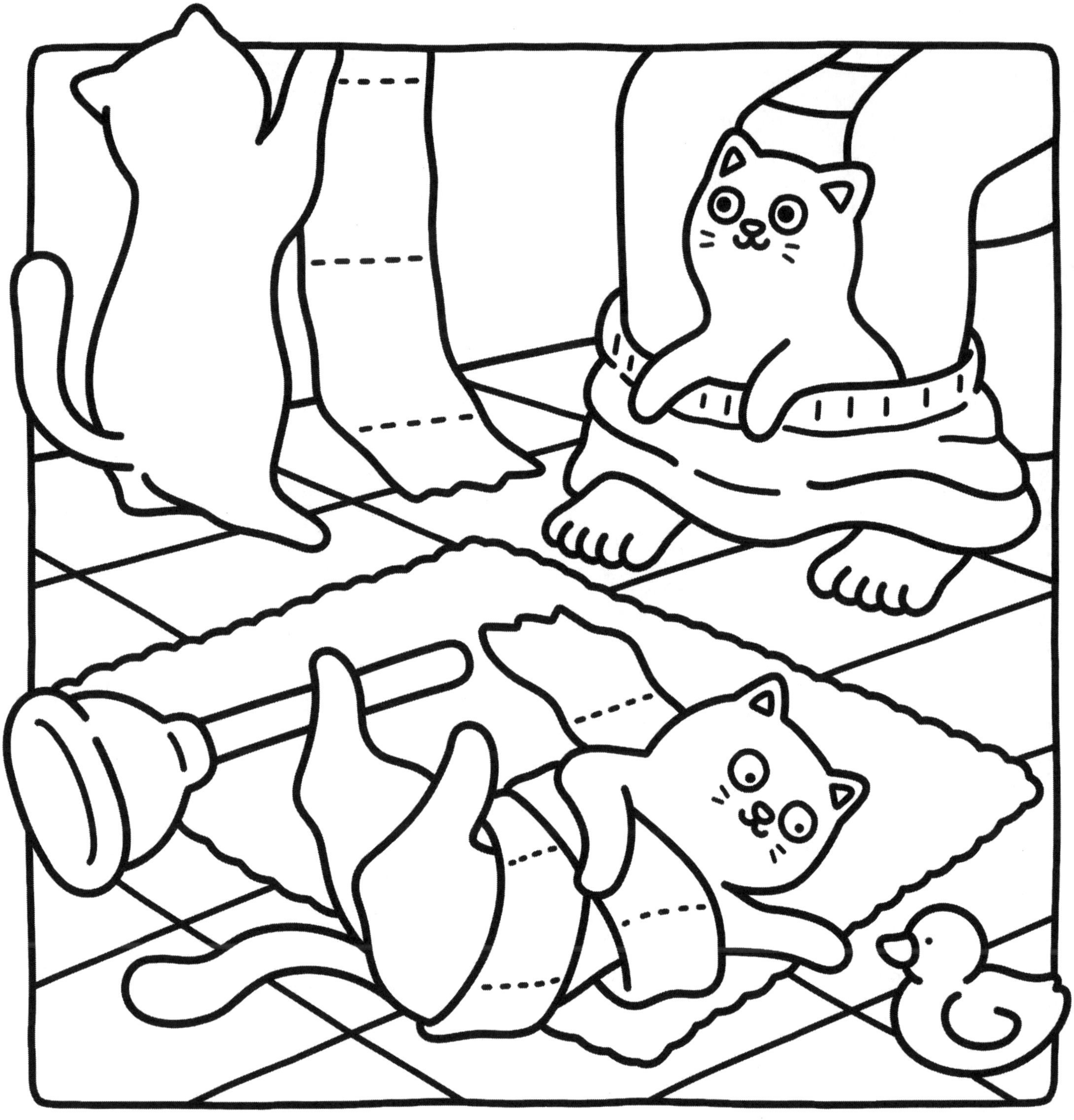

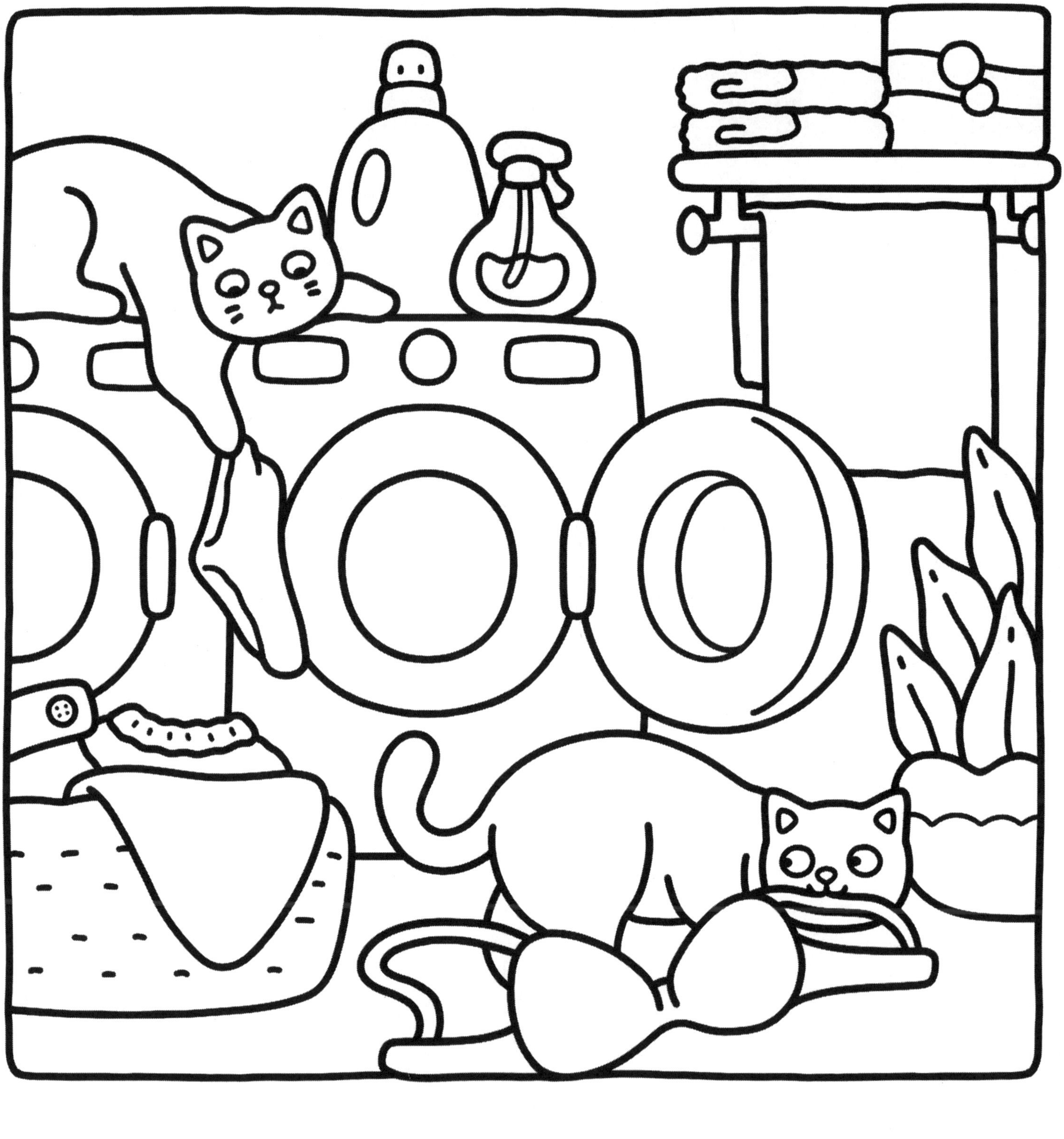

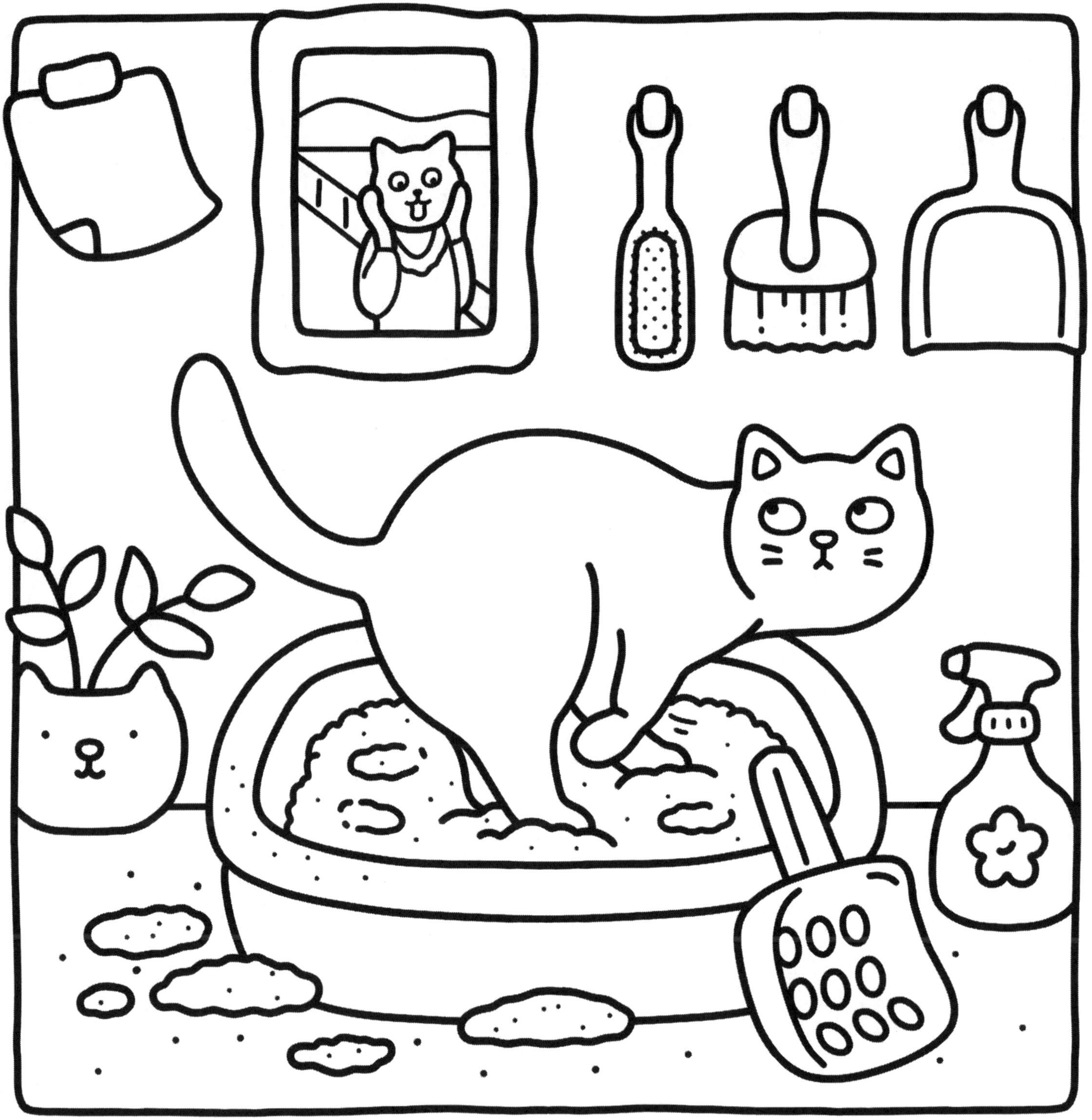

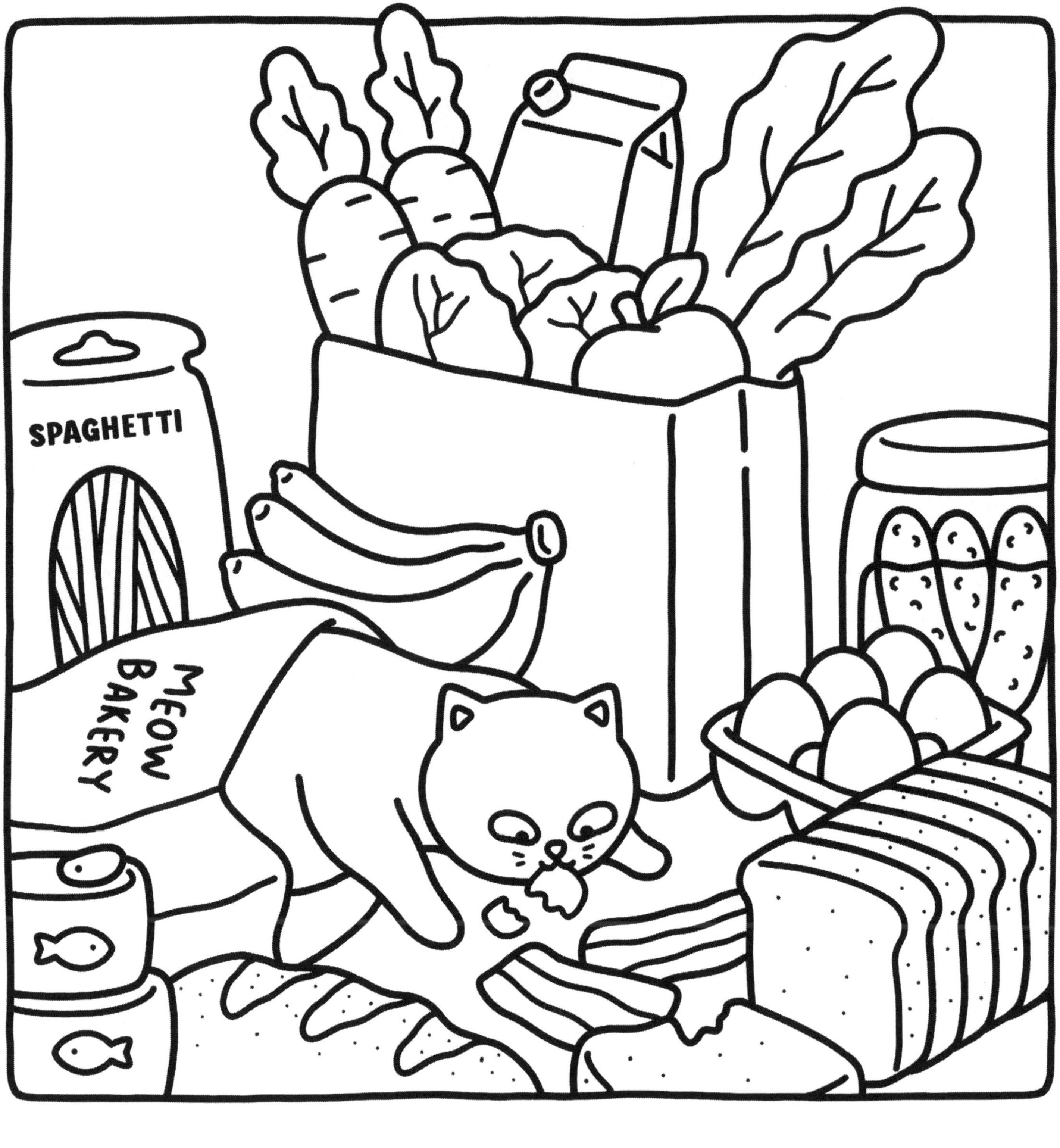
SPAGHETTI
MEOW BAKERY

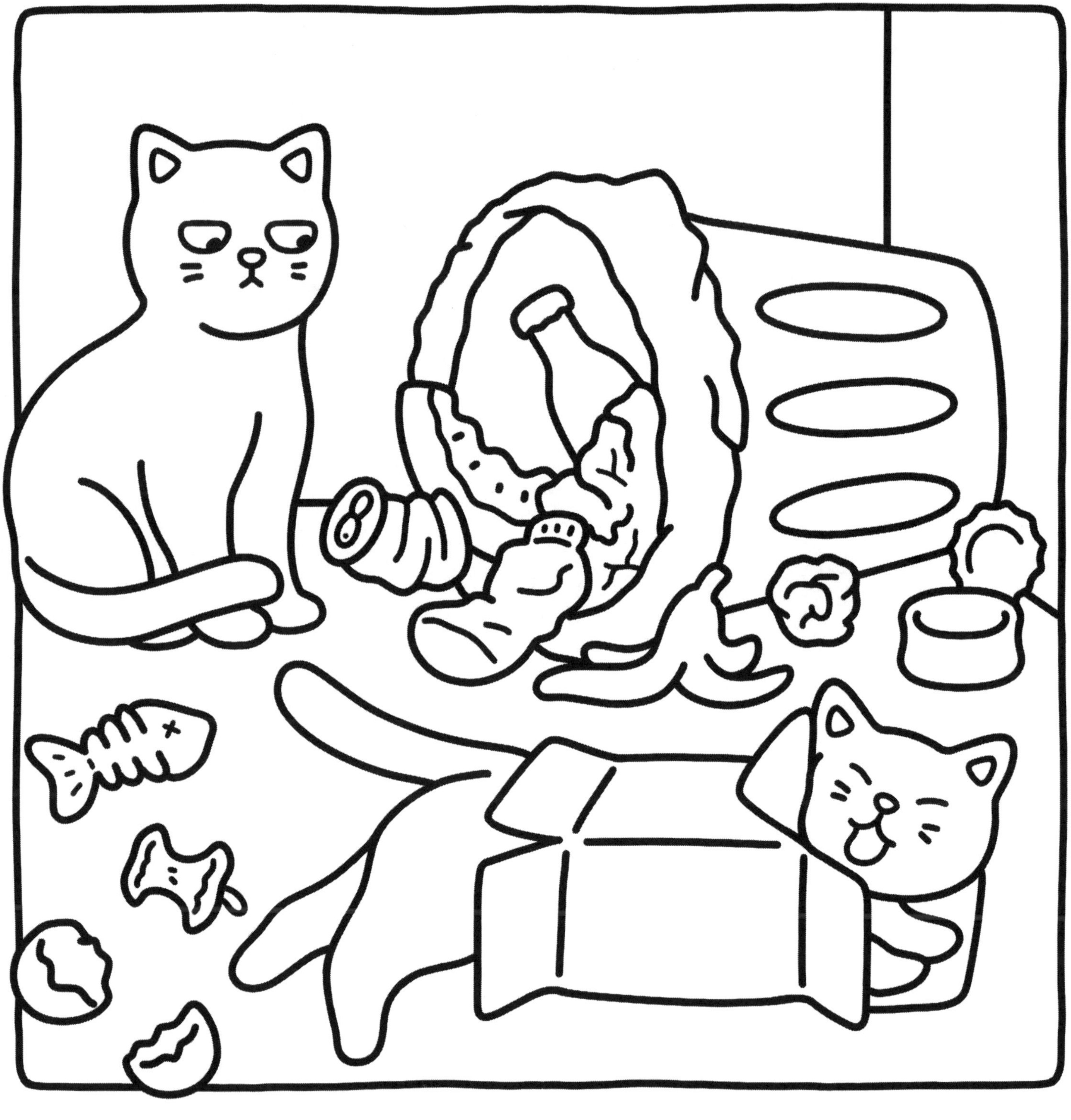

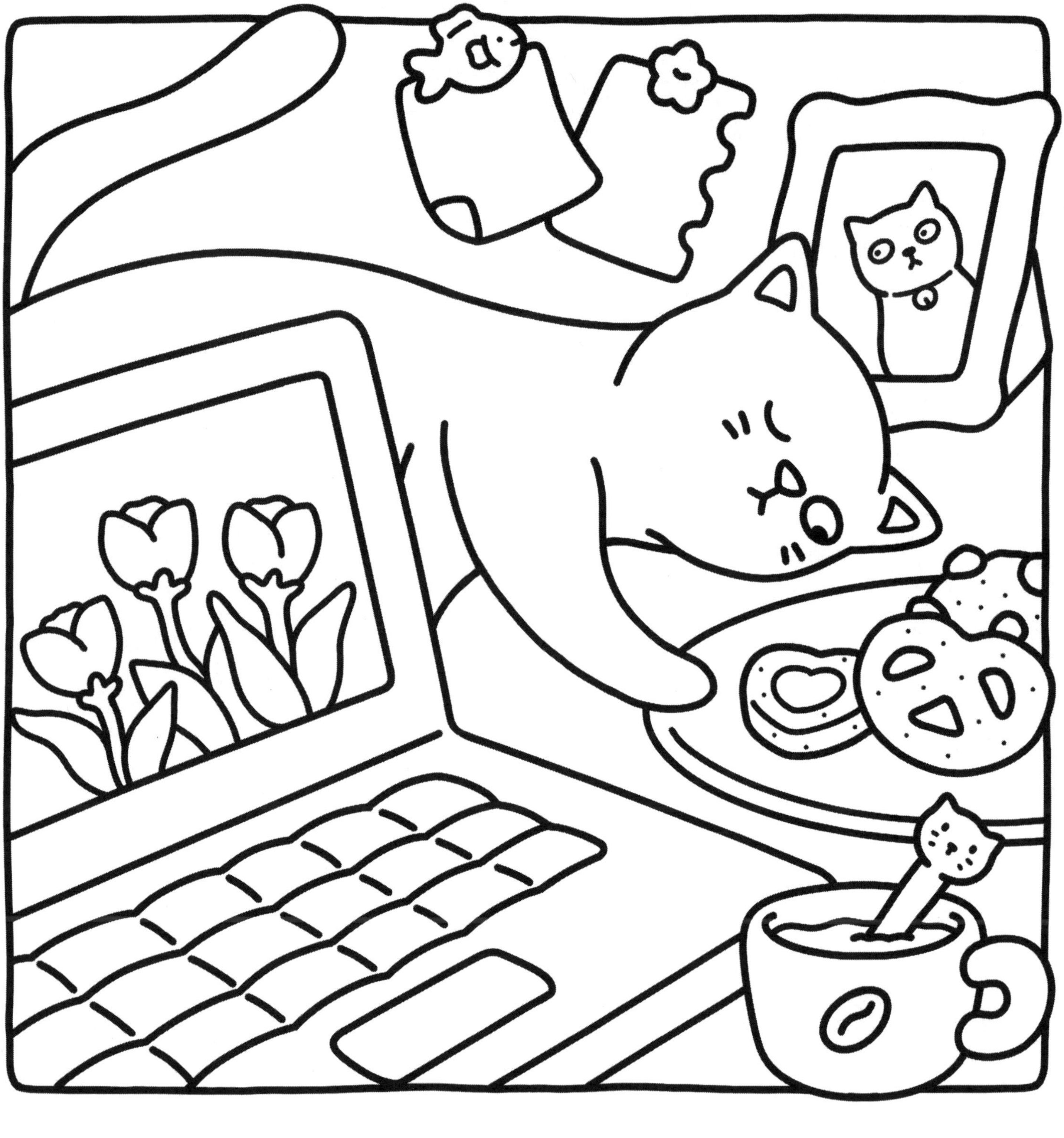

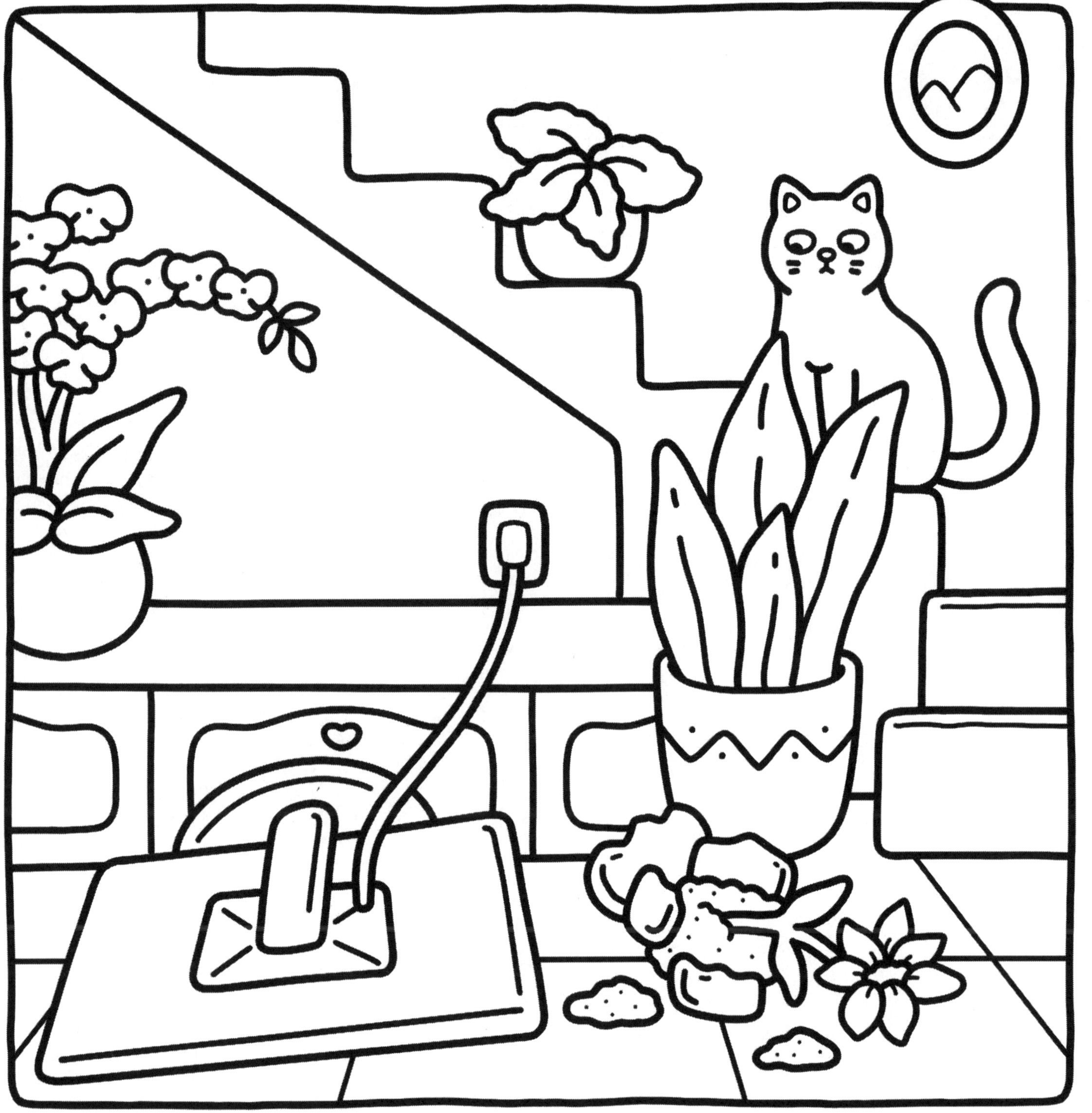

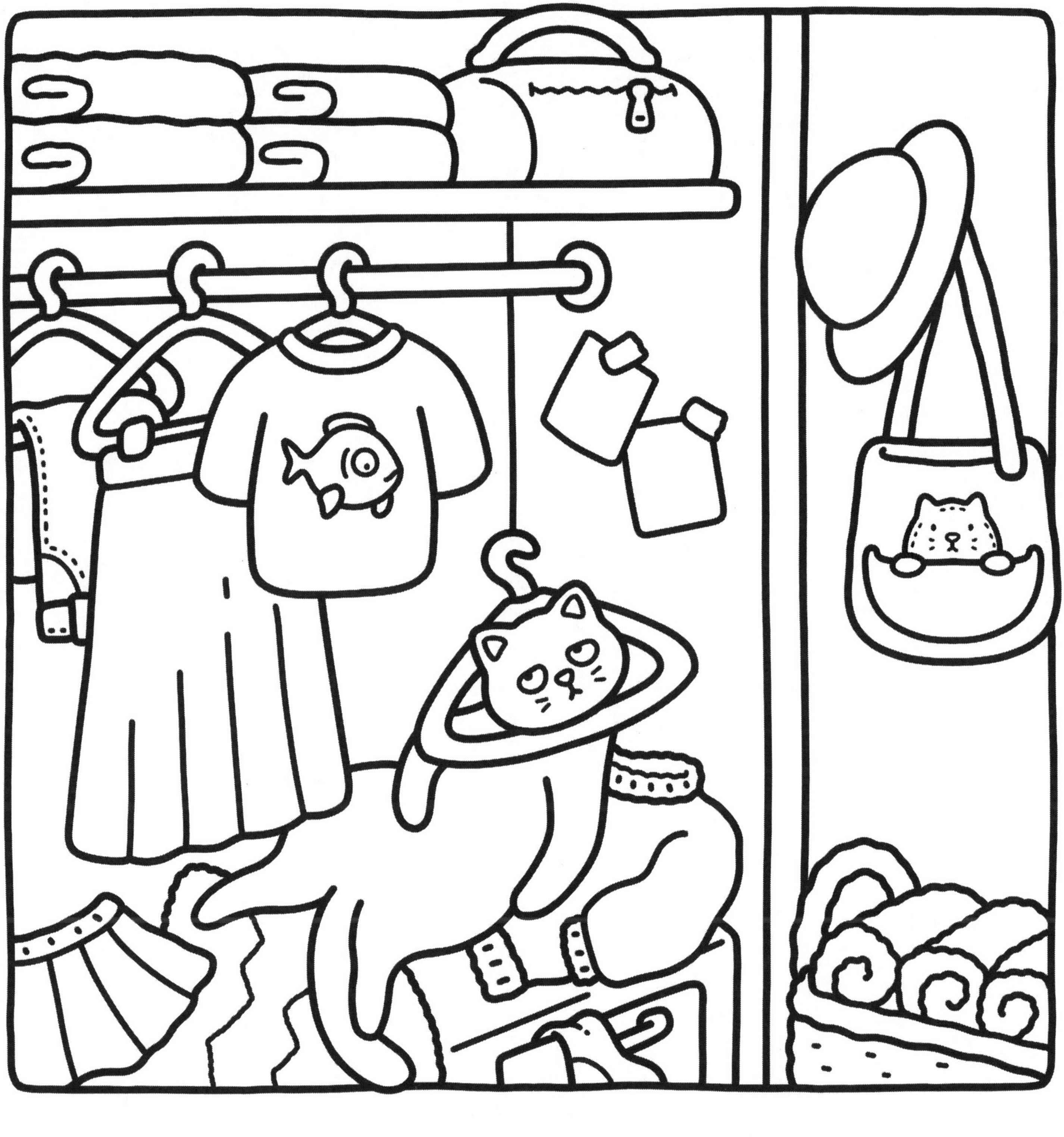

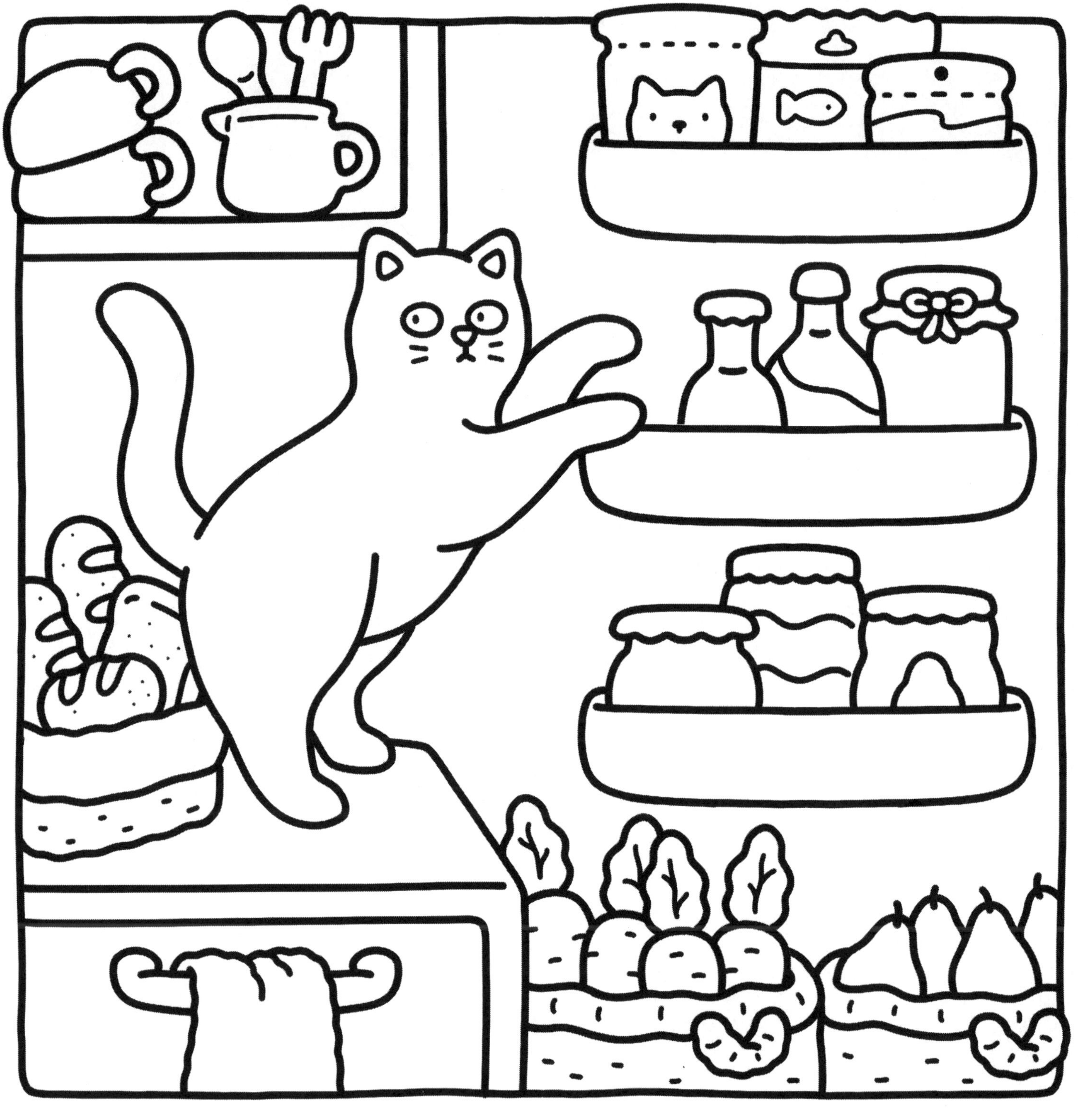

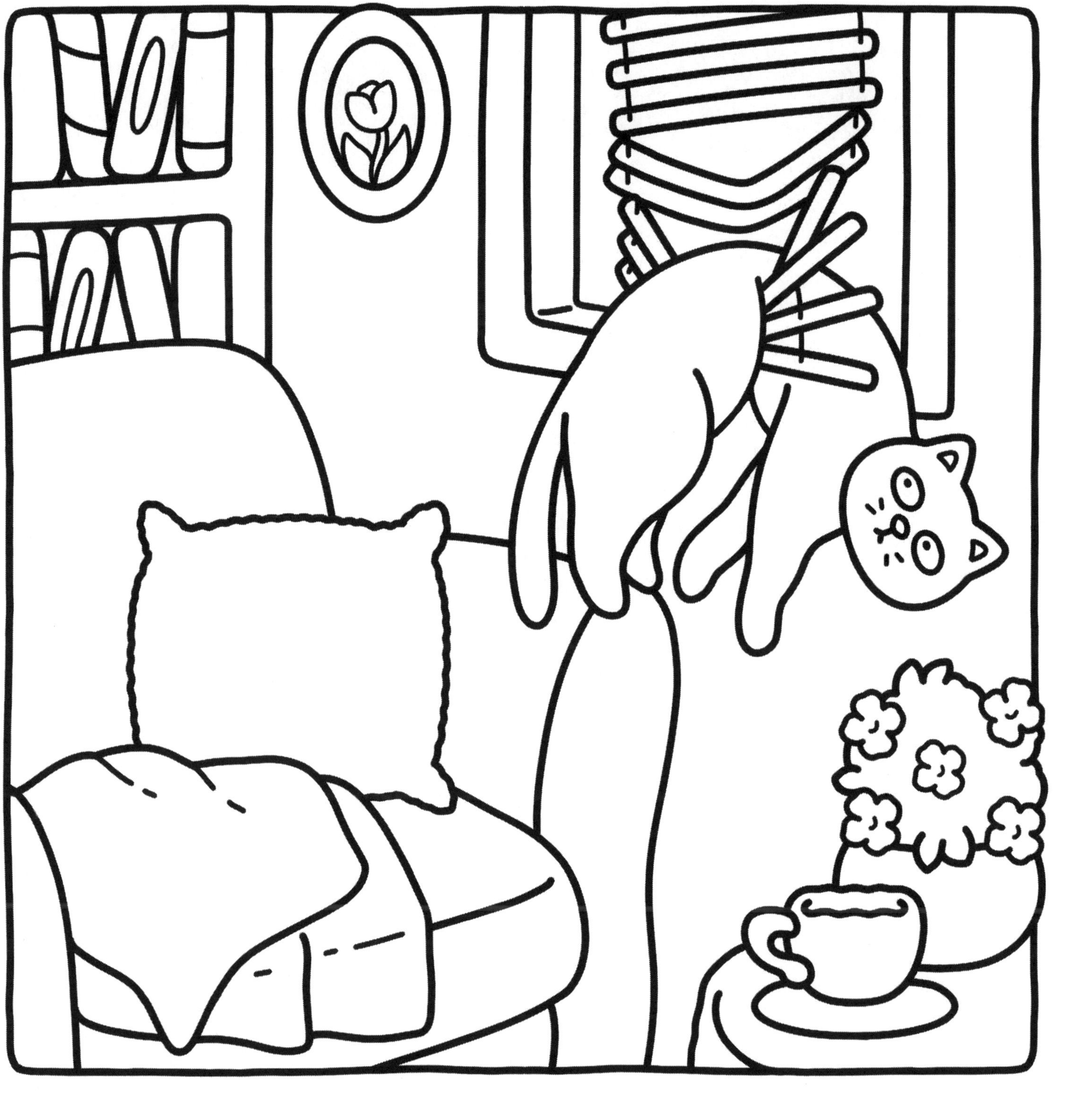

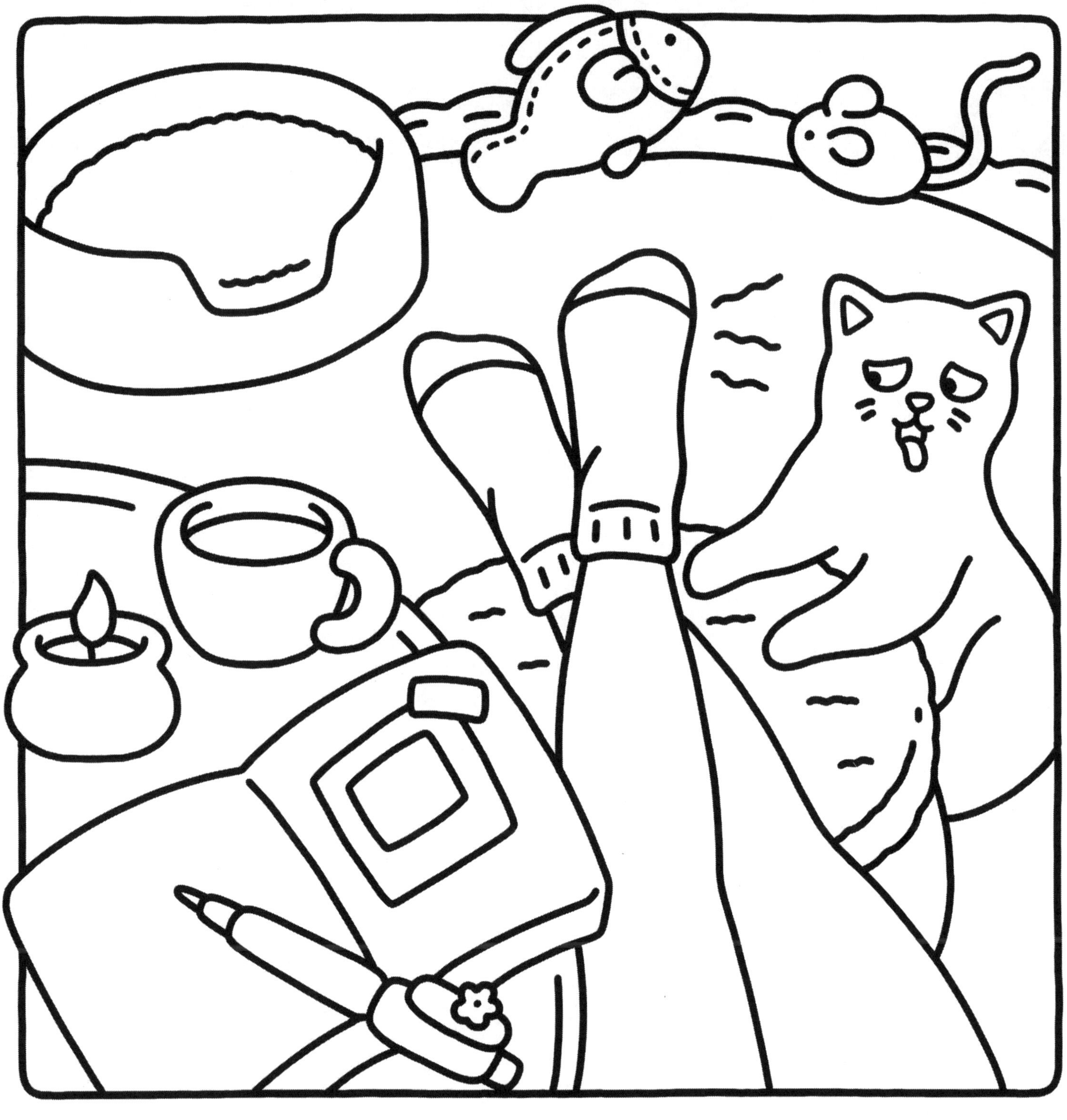

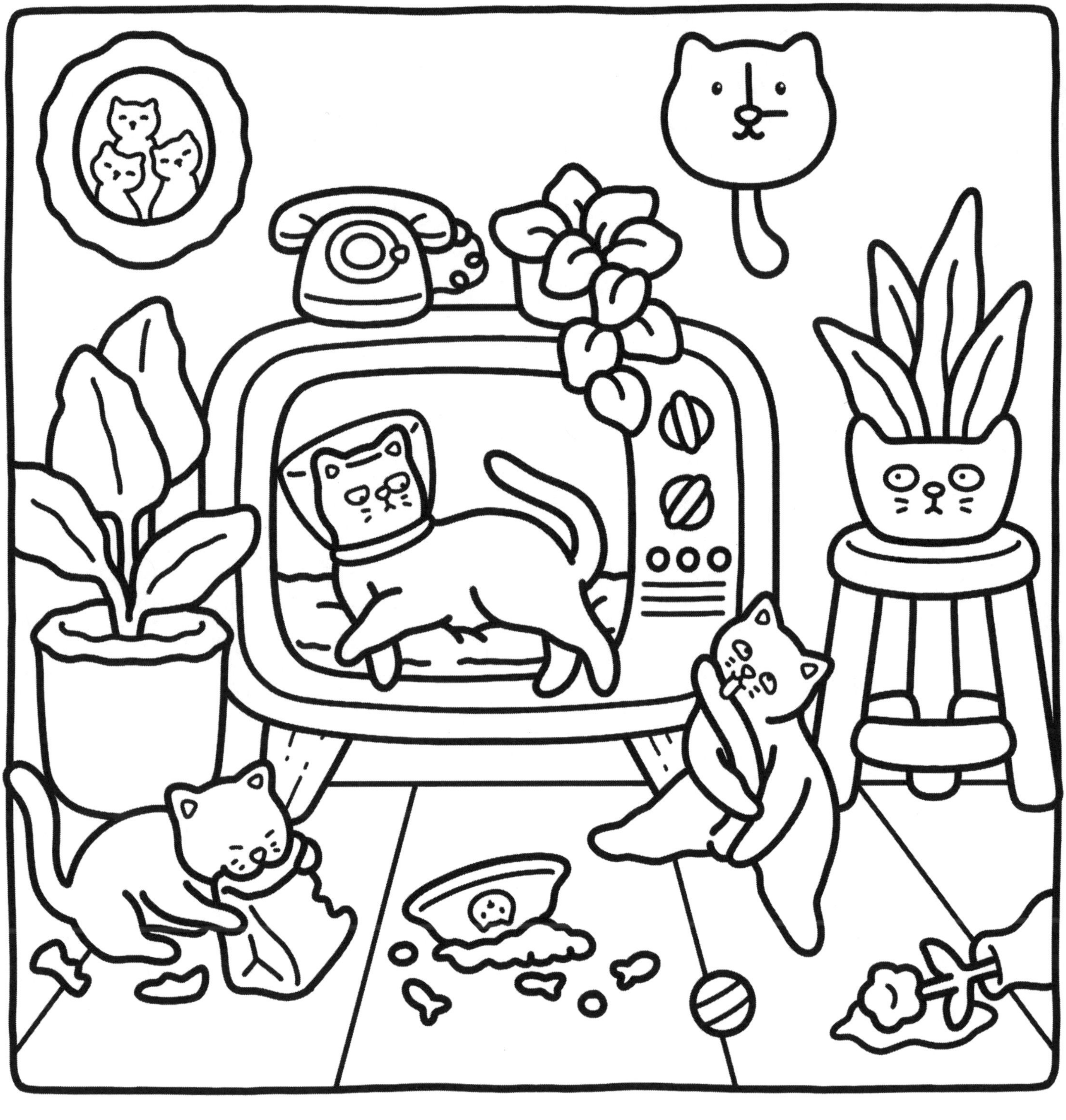